FAITH MISUNDERSTOOD

Reclaiming The Lost Science Of Belief

CGS ILLATHU

BlueRose ONE .com
Stories Matter
NewDelhi • London

BLUEROSE PUBLISHERS
India | U.K.

BlueRose ONE
Stories Matter
NewDelhi • London

For permissions requests or inquiries regarding this publication, please contact:

BLUEROSE PUBLISHERS
www.BlueRoseONE.com
info@bluerosepublishers.com
+91 8882 898 898
+4407342408967

ISBN: 978-93-7825-971-5

Cover Design: Deepak Katheria
Typesetting: Manisha Rawat

First Edition: April 2026

How to Read This Series

This series is not meant to be read quickly, sequentially, or conclusively.

Each book explores a distinct layer of human experience — awareness, growth, belief, responsibility, and integration. While the books are connected, they are written to stand on their own. You may enter the series at any point and leave at any point without loss.

What matters is not how much you read, but how much you recognize.

Some ideas may feel immediately familiar. Others may feel incomplete or unresolved. This is intentional. Understanding does not always arrive at the moment an idea is introduced; it often emerges later through reflection or lived experience.

You are not expected to agree with every perspective offered here. These books do not ask for belief, alignment, or acceptance. They invite observation.

If you find yourself pausing, rereading, or sitting with a chapter longer than expected, that is not resistance — it is often integration. Moving ahead before that integration occurs may make later ideas feel abstract or disconnected.

Each volume closes with a short reflection to help you assess your readiness to continue. These are not evaluations, but mirrors. They exist to support clarity, not progress.

This series unfolds as an exploration, not a conclusion. Some questions are intentionally left open, not because they lack answers, but because certain understandings cannot be carried forward prematurely.

Read at a pace that feels honest.
Pause where something feels unfinished.
Continue only when curiosity feels steady rather than urgent.

There is no final destination promised here — only a deepening of clarity, one step at a time.

If at any point you feel the impulse to defend or dismiss an idea before fully understanding it, pause. That reaction itself is part of what this book is exploring. This is not a challenge to your identity, beliefs, or intelligence—but an invitation to examine how those structures formed in the first place.

Series Preface

There has always been a quiet tension in the human story.

On one side, science—methodical, measurable, cautious—asking how things work.
On the other, faith—intuitive, experiential, symbolic—asking why they matter.

For centuries, these two were seen as adversaries. Yet they were never meant to be.

Long before laboratories and instruments existed, human beings were already observing patterns—within nature, within themselves, and within one another. They did not have equations, but they had attention. They did not have neuroscience, but they had lived awareness. What we now call "faith" was not blind belief; it was humanity's earliest attempt to make sense of consciousness, emotion, suffering, hope, and meaning.

Over time, something shifted.

What began as inner understanding slowly became external authority.
What began as lived insight hardened into doctrine. What began as guidance for awareness became systems of control, identity, and division.

At the same time, science progressed rapidly—but in narrowing its focus to what could be measured, it often dismissed what could only be experienced. Inner life became subjective. Consciousness became inconvenient. Meaning was reduced to chemistry, even as humans continued to live, love, fear, and search for purpose.

This series exists because that split is no longer sustainable.

The Next Leap of Evolution invited you to pause and observe—to notice your thoughts, emotions, patterns, and reactions without immediately judging or trying to fix them. It was not a book of answers, but a book of awareness. Awareness is always the first step, because without it, every belief—scientific or spiritual—operates unconsciously.

Faith Misunderstood begins where that awareness naturally leads.

It does not ask you to adopt a belief.
It does not ask you to reject science.
It does not ask you to follow a religion or abandon one.

Instead, it asks a different question:

What if faith was never meant to replace thinking—but to precede understanding?

In these pages, ancient teachings, prophets, sages, and spiritual traditions are approached not as supernatural anomalies, but as expressions of deeply integrated human consciousness—individuals who understood the mechanics of emotion, thought, memory, and perception long before modern language existed to describe them.

Their stories are revisited not as literal history to be defended, nor as superstition to be dismissed, but as **symbolic maps of the human inner world**—maps that psychology and neuroscience are only now beginning to redraw in modern terms.

This book also addresses why faith so often feels dangerous today:
why it has been used to justify fear, division, guilt, and control;

why intelligent, rational minds instinctively recoil from it; and why rejecting it entirely leaves a different kind of emptiness behind.

By the end of this volume, faith is no longer something to accept or reject.
It becomes something to understand.

And once something is truly understood, it loses its power to dominate—or to deceive.

That understanding leads naturally to a more confronting realization, explored in the next volume of the series:

If belief, thought, and emotion have always shaped human behavior unconsciously,
what happens when an individual learns to observe and regulate them consciously?

That question marks a threshold—

where understanding gives way to responsibility,

and awareness gives way to mastery.

There is no urgency in this journey.
No hierarchy of enlightenment.
No promise of certainty.

Only an invitation—to see more clearly, to carry less fear, and to engage with life from a place of grounded awareness rather than inherited assumption.

You are encouraged to move forward only if these ideas feel steady rather than exciting, clarifying rather than destabilizing. Integration never requires speed.

Clarity arrives when it is ready.

Prologue

Before Belief Became Religion

Before belief had a name, it had a purpose.

Long before scriptures, symbols, or institutions, human beings lived in a world that was vast, unpredictable, and often unforgiving. Survival depended not only on physical strength, but on the ability to make sense of uncertainty—of death, danger, nature, and the unknown movements within one's own mind.

Early humans did not separate inner experience from outer reality. Fear, awe, gratitude, hope, and despair were not abstract emotions; they were forces that determined whether a group stayed together, whether a child was protected, whether a tribe endured a harsh season or collapsed under panic.

What we now call *faith* was born in this space—not as blind belief, but as **meaning-making.**

When thunder shook the sky, when illness struck without warning, when death arrived without explanation, the human mind did what it still does today: it searched for patterns. Not out of ignorance, but out of necessity. A mind that cannot find meaning in uncertainty fractures under it.

Faith was the mind's earliest stabilizer.

It offered coherence where chaos threatened to overwhelm.
It offered continuity where mortality disrupted.
It offered reassurance where fear could otherwise turn inward and destroy.

In this sense, faith was never opposed to intelligence. It was intelligence—operating without the tools we now possess.

As human consciousness evolved, certain individuals developed a deeper capacity to observe the inner world. They noticed that fear could be softened through trust, that anger dissolved through compassion, that silence clarified thought, and that attention itself altered experience. These individuals became what history would later call sages, prophets, seers, and enlightened beings.

Their insights were not theoretical. They were lived.

But lived truth is fragile.

As generations passed, insight was retold as story. Story became teaching. Teaching became rule. And rule, when repeated without understanding, hardened into authority.

What was once experiential slowly became external. What was once guidance became commandment. What was once inward clarity became outward control.

Religion, in this form, was not created to deceive. It emerged as an attempt to preserve insight across time—yet preservation without understanding inevitably distorts the original message. Symbols replaced awareness. Obedience replaced inquiry. Identity replaced integration.

At the same time, another shift was taking place.

As science emerged and matured, it brought unprecedented clarity to the external world. Matter could be measured. Motion could be predicted. The universe could be mapped. Yet the inner world—the very domain faith once addressed—was increasingly dismissed as subjective, unreliable, or unscientific.

This created a false divide.

Faith, stripped of understanding, drifted into superstition and control.
Science, stripped of inner inquiry, drifted into reductionism and detachment.

Humanity inherited both fragments—and mistook them for complete truths.

This book stands at that fault line.

Not to defend religion or science,
nor to undermine either,
but to revisit the original human questions that gave rise to both.

What is belief?
Why does it shape behavior so powerfully?
How do thought, emotion, memory, and meaning influence biology, relationships, and societies?
And why did ancient teachings grasp these dynamics intuitively, while modern systems often struggle to integrate them?

Faith Misunderstood does not ask you to return to belief. It asks you to understand **why belief existed at all**—and what remains valuable once belief is no longer required.

By reframing faith through the lenses of psychology, neuroscience, and human evolution, this book attempts to restore what was lost when belief became doctrine and meaning became monopoly.

What remains is not faith as submission—but **faith as inner alignment**.

And once alignment is understood, the question is no longer *what to believe…*

…but what becomes possible when belief no longer controls you – and you're consciously shaping it.

Contents

Chapter 1
The Survival Brain And The Birth of Meaning

The human brain did not evolve to seek truth.
It evolved to ensure survival.

Long before humans questioned existence, morality, or purpose, the brain's primary task was simple: *detect threat, predict danger, and keep the body alive.* Every thought, emotion, and perception emerged from this fundamental requirement.

This is not a flaw in human design. It is its foundation.

Fear, vigilance, and pattern-recognition were not weaknesses of early humans; they were advantages. A mind that anticipated danger lived longer than one that waited for certainty. A mind that noticed patterns—even imperfect ones—was more likely to avoid harm than one that required proof.

Meaning emerged from this survival imperative.

When early humans encountered recurring uncertainty—storms, illness, predators, death—the brain sought coherence. Randomness is deeply destabilizing to the nervous system. A threat that can be named, explained, or symbolized becomes psychologically manageable, even if the explanation is incomplete.

This is where belief first took root.

Not as theology.
Not as obedience.
But as **cognitive stabilization**.

To believe that events followed intention—whether of nature, ancestors, or unseen forces—was not irrational. It reduced anxiety. It restored a sense of predictability. It allowed individuals and groups to function without being paralyzed by fear.

Modern psychology recognizes this instinct clearly.

The human nervous system cannot remain in prolonged uncertainty without cost. Chronic unpredictability activates stress responses, erodes trust, fragments attention, and destabilizes behavior. Meaning—any meaning—temporarily resolves that instability.

In this sense, belief was humanity's earliest psychological technology.

The Brain's Need for Narrative

Neuroscience now confirms what ancient cultures intuitively understood: the brain is a narrative-building organ.

It does not passively receive reality. It interprets it.

Sensory input is filtered, prioritized, and organized into stories that explain *what is happening, why it matters, and what should be done next.* These stories guide action far more powerfully than facts alone.

When reliable data is unavailable—as it was for most of human history—the brain fills gaps using emotion, memory, and imagination. This is not deception; it is adaptation.

A mind without narrative loses direction.
A mind without meaning loses motivation.
A mind without coherence collapses inward.

Faith, in its earliest form, functioned as a stabilizing narrative that aligned inner experience with outer reality. It gave people a way to endure suffering, explain loss, and maintain social cohesion.

Importantly, these narratives were rarely arbitrary. They were shaped by lived experience.

Storm gods emerged in storm-ridden regions. Fertility symbols emerged where survival depended on crops. Moral codes emerged where cooperation determined survival.

Belief systems reflected ecological and psychological realities, even when expressed symbolically.

Emotion Came Before Explanation

Modern thought often assumes that belief follows reasoning. In reality, the opposite is usually true.

Emotion precedes explanation.

The brain registers safety or threat before conscious thought arises. Only afterward does the mind construct a rationale to justify the feeling. This is why beliefs are so difficult to change through argument alone—because they are rooted in emotional memory, not logic.

Early humans did not "decide" to believe.
They *felt* their way into belief.

Fear demanded reassurance.
Grief demanded continuity.
Hope demanded possibility.

Faith addressed these needs directly.

Rituals calmed the nervous system.
Stories regulated collective emotion.
Symbols anchored memory across generations.

What looks primitive through a modern lens was, in fact, psychologically sophisticated.

Collective Survival and Shared Meaning

Belief was never purely individual. It was communal.

Groups that shared meaning coordinated better. They trusted one another more readily. They endured hardship with less fragmentation. Shared belief synchronized behavior long before language or law could do so effectively.

This is a crucial point often missed in modern critiques of faith.

Belief systems were not merely about explaining the world; they were about **holding groups together under pressure**. Cooperation required trust, and trust required shared understanding of reality—even if symbolic.

In this sense, faith functioned as social glue.

It aligned emotion, behavior, and expectation within a group, reducing internal conflict and increasing resilience. This collective coherence often mattered more than factual accuracy.

Evolution favors what works.

The Cost of Meaning—and Its Necessity

Of course, belief also carried risks.

When narratives hardened, when symbols replaced inquiry, when fear was manipulated rather than soothed, belief became a tool of control. But that distortion came later. It was not the origin.

To dismiss early faith as ignorance is to misunderstand the conditions under which human consciousness evolved.

The real question is not why humans believed—but why modern societies, despite advanced knowledge, still struggle with the same fears, divisions, and anxieties.

The answer is uncomfortable.

We have improved our explanations of the external world, but we have not evolved at the same pace in understanding the inner one.

The survival brain still governs behavior.
Emotion still precedes reason.
Meaning still shapes action more than facts.

The difference is that belief today often operates unconsciously, without the symbolic frameworks that once acknowledged its power.

This leaves modern humans informed—but fragmented.

A Necessary Foundation

Understanding faith as a survival-driven response is not an excuse for dogma. It is a foundation for clarity.

Until belief is understood psychologically, it will continue to operate invisibly—shaping decisions, relationships, politics, and identity without conscious awareness.

This book does not ask you to revive faith.

It asks you to **recognize the conditions that gave rise to it**, so you can see where those same mechanisms are still at work within you.

Only then can belief be transformed from an unconscious driver into a conscious choice.

And only then can the journey move from survival… to awareness.

Where Meaning Lives

If belief stabilized early humans through shared meaning, the next question is inevitable:

Where did that meaning reside—and how did it survive beyond a single lifetime?

The answer lies in memory—not only individual memory, but emotional and collective memory that outlives those who first experienced it.

This is where belief began to take form as something enduring.

And this is where the first gods emerged.

Chapter 2
Memory, Emotion, And The First Gods

Meaning does not survive through logic alone. It survives through **memory charged with emotion**.

Modern neuroscience is unequivocal on this point: experiences paired with strong emotion are remembered longer, transmitted more reliably, and influence behavior more deeply than neutral information. Memory is not a recording device—it is a *selective reinforcement system.*

Early humans did not preserve meaning by writing equations or documenting observations. They preserved it by **encoding experience into emotionally resonant symbols and stories.**

This is where the first gods appeared—not as beings descending from the sky, but as **containers of memory.**

Memory as the Original Archive

The human brain stores memory in layers.

- **Declarative memory** holds facts and events
- **Emotional memory** stores fear, safety, attachment, loss
- **Procedural memory** encodes habits and responses

What persists across generations is rarely factual detail. What persists is **emotional pattern**.

This is why a community can forget the original event yet retain the fear, reverence, or gratitude associated with it. Over time, emotion seeks form—and form becomes symbol.

Gods, spirits, ancestors, heavens, and hells were not random inventions. They were **symbolic stabilizers**, ensuring that emotionally important lessons were not lost.

Gods as Emotional Archetypes, Not External Beings

Across cultures, deities display strikingly consistent characteristics:

- Wrathful gods emerge in violent, unstable environments
- Protective gods emerge in fragile survival conditions
- Fertility gods arise where reproduction and agriculture determine survival
- Moral gods appear when group size exceeds personal familiarity

This consistency is not coincidence.

It reflects how **collective emotional memory shapes belief structures.**

What religion later described as divine attributes—anger, compassion, judgment, forgiveness—are recognizable today as **human emotional states amplified and externalized**.

In psychological terms, early humans **projected internal emotional forces outward**, creating shared symbols that allowed groups to regulate those forces collectively.

☐ **God as Judge and Moral law**

- **Christianity:** God as moral judge
- **Islam:** Judgment and accountability (Hisab)
- **Hinduism:** Dharma as universal law
- **Buddhism:** Moral causality through Karma
- **Sikhism:** Living in alignment with Hukam

This is not primitive thinking. It is *distributed emotional regulation.*

Scripture as Symbolic Compression

When memory must travel across generations without distortion, it cannot rely on explanation alone. It must be **compressed into imagery**.

This is why religious texts are filled with metaphor.

Let us look at a few examples—not as belief claims, but as symbolic representations now validated through science and psychology.

Light vs Darkness — Awareness vs Unconsciousness

Almost every religious tradition equates light with truth, clarity, or divinity—and darkness with ignorance or evil.

▢ Light and Darkness

- **Christianity (Bible):** "I am the light of the world." (John 8:12)
- **Islam (Qur'an):** "Allah is the Light of the heavens and the earth." (24:35)
- **Hinduism (Upanishads):** Tamas (ignorance) and Sattva (clarity)
- **Buddhism:** Avidyā (ignorance) as the root of suffering
- **Sikhism (Guru Granth Sahib):** "From darkness, I am brought into light."

This is not moral judgment. It is neurological.

Modern neuroscience shows that awareness literally involves **increased neural integration and activation**. Clarity corresponds with coherence across brain regions. Confusion, fear, and dissociation correlate with reduced integration.

"Walking in darkness" symbolizes operating unconsciously—driven by unexamined fear and impulse. "Seeing the light" symbolizes insight—sudden integration of understanding.

This metaphor persists because it maps cleanly onto lived experience.

Heaven and Hell — Psychological States, Not Destinations

Scriptures describe heaven as peace, abundance, unity—and hell as torment, isolation, suffering.

Psychology now describes the same states without metaphysics.

A regulated nervous system experiences safety, connection, and meaning.
A chronically dysregulated one experiences anxiety, rage, despair, and fragmentation.

People do not go to these states after death. They **enter them repeatedly while alive**.

▢ **Heaven and Hell**

- **Christianity (Bible):** "The kingdom of God is within you." (Luke 17:21)
- **Islam (Qur'an):** Paradise (Jannah) and Hell (Jahannam) described as states tied to the heart and deeds
- **Hinduism:** Swarga and Naraka as experiential realms
- **Buddhism:** Heavenly and hell realms as states of consciousness
- **Sikhism:** Union or separation from Naam (divine awareness)

Heaven and hell endured as symbols because they encoded emotional realities that language alone could not preserve.

Sin and Purity — Cognitive Dissonance and Integration

The concept of sin is often misunderstood as moral condemnation. Symbolically, it refers to **inner misalignment**.

When actions contradict values, the nervous system experiences tension—what psychology calls cognitive dissonance. Chronic dissonance erodes well-being, coherence, and self-trust.

▢ Sin, Karma and Conditioning

- **Christianity:** Sin as separation from God
- **Islam:** Accountability for actions (Akhirah)
- **Hinduism:** Karma as consequence of action
- **Buddhism:** Samskara as mental conditioning
- **Sikhism:** Actions aligned or misaligned with Hukam (natural order)

"Purity" symbolizes alignment—when thought, emotion, and action move together.

This is why confession, repentance, and atonement were emotionally relieving long before they were moralized. They restored *psychological integration.*

The Fall — Loss of Innocent Awareness

The story of the fall—from Eden, from grace, from unity—appears across traditions.

Symbolically, it reflects a transition modern psychology recognizes well: the shift from **pre-reflective awareness to self-consciousness.**

Once humans became capable of self-evaluation, comparison, and anticipation, innocence was lost. Anxiety was born. Shame became possible. Identity fragmented.

The "fall" was not moral failure.
It was the **cost of consciousness**.

▢ The Fall and Loss of Innocence

- **Christianity (Genesis):** The Fall after knowledge of good and evil
- **Islam:** Humanity's descent after awareness and choice
- **Hinduism (Vedanta):** Maya — identification with the limited self
- **Buddhism:** Emergence of ego (atta) as the root of suffering
- **Sikhism:** Separation from Naam through ego (haumai)

Memory That Outlives Individuals

Some memories are too large to belong to a single person.

Trauma, gratitude, displacement, survival, near-extinction—these experiences shape communities. Today, epigenetics shows that stress and safety can influence gene expression across generations, without altering DNA sequences themselves.

This does not require mysticism. It requires recognition that **biology remembers experience**.

▢ Blessings, Curses and Ancestral Continuity

- **Christianity:** Generational blessings and sins
- **Islam:** Lineage, responsibility, and inherited consequences
- **Hinduism:** Pitru Rin (ancestral obligation)
- **Buddhism:** Intergenerational conditioning
- **Sikhism:** Inherited tendencies refined through awareness

Religious emphasis on lineage, ancestry, blessing, curse, and inheritance symbolized this long before laboratories could observe it.

Faith preserved what science could not yet measure.

Why These Symbols Endured

Symbols endure when they remain *experientially true.*

They fail when taken literally.

Religion fractured when metaphor was mistaken for fact and story replaced inquiry. Science fractured when inner experience was dismissed because it could not be quantified.

Faith Misunderstood exists in the space between these failures.

To recognize that ancient teachings encoded psychological truth is not to romanticize the past. It is to acknowledge that

human consciousness has always been the same instrument—only the language has evolved.

Where Meaning Lives

Meaning lives where emotion and memory intersect.

It survives not because it is correct, but because it is *felt.*

The next question follows naturally:

If memory and emotion shaped the first gods, what kind of minds were capable of seeing beyond those symbols?

That question leads us to the individuals history calls prophets, sages, and enlightened beings—not as divine exceptions, but as **fully integrated humans**.

Chapter 3
Were Prophets Superhuman — Or Fully Integrated Humans?

History remembers certain individuals differently.

They are called prophets, sages, messengers, enlightened ones, avatars. Their words are preserved, repeated, ritualized. Their lives are surrounded by reverence, controversy, and often fear. Over time, they are lifted out of the human frame and placed beyond it.

This separation has had an unintended consequence.

By making these figures superhuman, humanity lost the ability to understand how they saw what they saw — and therefore lost access to the very capacities they were pointing toward.

The question this chapter asks is deliberately simple:

Were these individuals fundamentally different from other humans — or were they simply more integrated?

Integration, Not Exception

Modern psychology offers a useful lens here.

A well-integrated human being is one in whom:

- Thought is not constantly hijacked by fear
- Emotion is felt without overwhelming reason
- Attention is stable rather than fragmented
- Identity is flexible rather than defensive

Such a mind is not empty or passive. It is coherent.

Neuroscience shows that coherence across brain regions correlates with clarity, compassion, creativity, and insight. When internal conflict reduces, perception sharpens. When fear subsides, attention expands.

What religious traditions later described as divine perception aligns closely with what modern science recognizes as **highly regulated, low-noise cognition.**

These individuals did not access another world. They perceived this one more clearly.

Insight and the Risk of Instability

There is a reason societies have always been uneasy around such people.

A sudden increase in insight — without grounding — can destabilize the mind. Psychology recognizes this today in the thin boundary between profound insight and psychological breakdown.

When meaning floods consciousness faster than identity can adapt, disorientation follows. The world feels unreal. Language fails. The individual may appear incoherent or threatening to others.

This is why many prophetic narratives include periods of:

- Withdrawal
- Silence
- Wilderness
- Fasting
- Solitude

These were not acts of mysticism. They were **regulatory phases** — allowing the nervous system to stabilize while perception expanded.

Insight without integration fractures.
Integration without insight stagnates.

The figures remembered most clearly were those who achieved *both.*

▢ Withdrawal and Preparation

- **Christianity:** Jesus' forty days in the wilderness
- **Islam:** Muhammad's retreats to the cave of Hira
- **Buddhism:** Siddhartha's prolonged meditation
- **Hinduism:** Sages entering vanaprastha (forest retreat)
- **Sikhism:** Guru Nanak's extended contemplative journeys

Why They Threatened Power

Integrated individuals do not rely on fear, status, or division to influence others. This makes them inherently destabilizing to systems built on control.

They do not demand belief.
They do not enforce identity.
They speak from experience rather than authority.

This is why they were often misunderstood, resisted, or eliminated — not because their message was violent, but because it bypassed existing hierarchies.

Fear-based systems require dependency.
Clarity dissolves dependency.

▢ Resistance to Prophets

- **Christianity:** Jesus executed as a political threat
- **Islam:** Early persecution of Muhammad and his followers
- **Judaism:** Prophets rejected by kings and institutions
- **Buddhism:** Opposition from entrenched priestly classes
- **Sikhism:** Martyrdom of Sikh Gurus under imperial rule

Language as the Last Limitation

One of the most misunderstood aspects of prophetic teaching is language itself.

These individuals were describing **inner states**, not external geography. But language is inherently symbolic, and listeners interpret symbols through their own level of awareness.

This is why teachings appear paradoxical, poetic, or contradictory.

"Die before you die."
"The kingdom is within you."
"Neti, neti." (Not this, not this.)

These were not riddles meant to confuse. They were attempts to point beyond conceptual thinking — something language struggles to do.

▢ Teaching Through Paradox

- **Christianity:** Parables and contradictions
- **Islam (Sufism):** "I searched for God and found only myself"
- **Hinduism (Upanishads):** Neti, neti
- **Buddhism:** Koans
- **Sikhism:** Poetry over doctrine

Compassion as a Byproduct, Not a Commandment

One of the most consistent traits across these figures is compassion.

Not sentimental kindness — but clarity-driven compassion. When fear no longer dominates perception, hostility loses its grip. When identity loosens, empathy becomes natural.

This is why teachings emphasized love, forgiveness, nonviolence, and service — not as moral obligations, but as expressions of an integrated mind.

Compassion was not taught.
It *emerged.*

Why They Were Deified

After their deaths, something predictable happened.

Societies, unable to replicate their clarity, preserved their words instead. Practices turned into rituals. Insight turned into instruction. Over time, the person became sacred — not to honor their humanity, but to protect society from the discomfort of comparison.

Deification was safer than imitation.

If they were divine, no one else had to become clear.

▢ From Human to Divine

- **Christianity:** Son of God
- **Hinduism:** Avatars
- **Buddhism:** Enlightened Buddha-nature
- **Islam:** Seal of the Prophets
- **Sikhism:** Gurus as divine channels

Where We Still See This Today

If integrated perception were rare or inaccessible, history would have ended with prophets.

But it didn't.

We still recognize this quality instinctively — even when we don't have language for it.

You see it in people who remain calm under pressure, not because they are detached, but because they are internally steady. You notice it in those who listen without preparing a response, who act without needing validation, who speak with clarity rather than urgency.

They are not always spiritual.
They are rarely dramatic.
They often go unnoticed.

Yet their presence changes the emotional climate around them.

These individuals exist in ordinary roles.

A teacher who doesn't humiliate, yet commands respect.
A leader who doesn't divide yet influences deeply.
A parent who doesn't control, yet creates safety.
A doctor, counsellor, or mentor whose calm steadies others before any advice is given.

Nothing about them appears supernatural.

And that is precisely the point.

What distinguishes them is not belief, intelligence, or moral superiority.

It is **integration.**

Their thoughts are not constantly at war with their emotions. Their emotions are not suppressed or indulged — they are understood. Their identity is not brittle. Their attention is not perpetually hijacked by fear or approval-seeking.

As a result, they see more clearly — not because they know more, but because less is **distorting their perception.**

Society struggles to place such people.

When they appear outside established systems, they are often labelled "idealistic," "naïve," or "unrealistic." When their clarity exceeds what the surrounding structure can accommodate, they may be marginalized, misunderstood, or quietly resisted.

And when their insight arrives faster than their ability to integrate it — which happens more often than history admits — they may appear unstable.

This is where the line between wisdom and breakdown becomes uncomfortably thin.

Modern culture does not mythologize such individuals as prophets.

It does something else.

It pathologizes them.
Or idolizes them.
Or consumes them as inspiration — without imitation.

Genius is celebrated. Stability is expected. Integration is rarely cultivated.

The ancient world responded differently.

When clarity appeared, it was elevated beyond humanity — turned divine, sacred, untouchable. This preserved the message, but at a cost: it quietly removed responsibility from the rest of humanity.

If they were gods, no one else had to become clear.

Modern society makes the opposite mistake.

It insists everyone be functional — but rarely teaches them how to be integrated.

The truth sits uncomfortably between these two extremes.

Integrated human functioning is neither mystical nor guaranteed. It is possible, uneven, fragile, and deeply dependent on emotional grounding, safety, and time.

When it is supported, it leads to clarity and compassion. When it is rushed or unsupported, it can lead to fragmentation.

This distinction matters.

Because it explains why some individuals return from insight grounded — while others do not.

And that distinction is where we must now turn.

What Was Lost — and What Remains

When prophets were lifted beyond humanity, their central message quietly disappeared:

What is possible for one integrated human is possible, in degrees, for others.

Not instantly.
Not identically.
But organically.

This does not diminish their contribution. It restores its relevance.

Where This Leaves Us

Faith misunderstood these individuals as exceptions. Religion preserved their words but not their method. Science dismissed their experience but now measures its effects.

This book exists to reconnect those threads.

And it leads to a deeper, more uncomfortable question — one this volume will not yet answer fully:

If clarity, compassion, and insight are human capacities, what happens when an individual takes responsibility for cultivating them consciously?

That question marks the boundary of this book.

It is also the threshold of the next.

Chapter 4
Revelation, Insight, And The Thin Line with Psychosis

Not every mind that sees beyond the familiar is awakened. And not every mind that breaks under pressure is ill.

The distinction matters.

Throughout history, moments of profound insight have often been accompanied by confusion, withdrawal, emotional volatility, or altered perception. Religious traditions recorded these moments as revelation. Modern psychology often encounters them as crisis.

Both perspectives are observing the same phenomenon from different angles.

The human mind is not designed to absorb sudden, large-scale reorganization without consequence.

What Insight Actually Is

Insight is not the acquisition of new information. It is the **reorganization of existing perception**.

When deeply held assumptions collapse at once, the mind experiences a rapid shift in meaning. This can feel liberating, terrifying, or both. Familiar reference points dissolve. Identity loosens. The sense of self becomes unstable.

Neuroscience associates such moments with intense neural re-patterning. Psychology recognizes them as **meaning-making threshold events.**

Handled gradually, they lead to growth.
Handled abruptly, they overwhelm.

This is the line where revelation and breakdown begin to resemble one another.

Why Sudden Clarity Can Be Dangerous

The nervous system requires stability to integrate change.

When insight arrives faster than emotional regulation can accommodate, the system enters overload. Sleep is disrupted. Thoughts accelerate. Boundaries blur. The world may feel unreal or excessively meaningful.

In religious language, this was described as being "possessed," "called," or "chosen."
In psychological language, it may resemble dissociation, mania, or psychosis.

Neither label captures the full picture.

The difference is not in the content of the experience — but in **whether the individual can return to grounded functioning**.

▢ Sudden Insight Across Traditions

- **Christianity:** Paul's blinding vision on the road to Damascus
- **Islam:** Muhammad's first revelation accompanied by fear and disorientation.
- **Buddhism:** Siddhartha's confrontation with suffering before awakening.
- **Hinduism:** Arjuna's overwhelm during Krishna's revelation.
- **Sikhism:** Guru Nanak's disappearance before his insight

Integration Is the Missing Step

Religious traditions that endured understood something subtle: insight alone was not enough.

This is why revelation narratives are often followed by long periods of:

- Silence
- Ethical refinement
- Service
- Teaching
- Return to ordinary life.

These phases were not optional. They were **integration processes**.

A mind that cannot function in ordinary reality is not liberated — it is fragmented.

True insight increases one's capacity to engage with life, not escape it.

Why Modern Systems Struggle Here

Modern psychology is cautious for good reason.

Unintegrated insight can cause real harm — to individuals and those around them. Romanticizing breakdowns as awakening risks neglect, misdiagnosis, and abandonment.

At the same time, purely suppressing or pathologizing all altered states ignores the mind's capacity for genuine reorganization and growth.

The discomfort arises because modern systems often treat:

- Stability as the goal
- Insight as a risk

Ancient systems often treated:

- Insight as the goal
- Stability as a responsibility

Both perspectives are incomplete on their own.

▢ Safeguards Emphasized in Traditions

- **Christianity:** Discernment and humility
- **Islam:** Gradual revelation over years
- **Buddhism:** The Middle Path
- **Hinduism:** Guru–disciple grounding
- **Sikhism:** Householder life, not withdrawal

The Role of Emotion in Recovery

What stabilizes insight is not intellect — it is **emotion**.

Safety, trust, love, and belonging allow the nervous system to settle. Without these, insight becomes isolating and threatening. This is why communities mattered so deeply in spiritual traditions — and why isolation often worsens breakdown.

When emotional grounding is restored, perception clarifies. What once felt overwhelming becomes intelligible.

This is not spirituality.
It is regulation.

Why Some Never Return

Some individuals never reintegrate.

This does not make their insight false — but it makes it unusable. A vision that cannot be lived cannot guide others. History remembers those who returned with clarity, not those who remained lost within it.

Awakening is not escape from humanity.
It is **return to it with less fear**.

How This Edge Appears in Ordinary Lives

Most people who come close to this edge never think of themselves as spiritual, visionary, or awakened.

They are ordinary individuals who, at some point, encounter a rapid internal shift.

It might follow loss, illness, intense stress, creative immersion, prolonged isolation, or sudden clarity. Something loosens.

Long-held assumptions collapse. Thoughts accelerate. Meaning floods perception faster than it can be organized.

To the person experiencing it, the world feels sharper, louder, more connected — and less stable.

To those around them, the change is unsettling.

In modern life, these moments rarely arrive with context.

There is no shared language for sudden insight. No collective understanding of how meaning reorganizes perception. No recognized phase for integration.

What *is* recognized is deviation from baseline functioning.

If the individual continues to work, speak coherently, and meet expectations, the experience is ignored or quietly self-managed. If they falter — sleep less, speak differently, withdraw, or express unusual connections — concern follows quickly.

The system responds to *disruption*, not to *depth*.

This creates a dangerous simplification.

Anything that destabilizes function is treated as pathology. Anything that restores function is treated as recovery.

But function alone does not distinguish integration from suppression.

Many people return to productivity without ever integrating what they saw. Others lose function precisely because integration was never supported.

The difference is not willpower or intelligence.
It is **regulation**.

You see this most clearly in creative and reflective individuals.

Writers, researchers, artists, entrepreneurs, therapists, and thinkers often operate close to this boundary. Their work requires immersion, prolonged attention, and tolerance for ambiguity — the same conditions under which insight accelerates.

When emotional grounding is present, this produces originality and depth.
When grounding is absent, the same process produces fragmentation.

Modern culture praises output but rarely protects integration.

What makes this especially difficult is that early insight often feels energizing.

Sleep reduces. Ideas multiply. Connections appear everywhere. Confidence rises — sometimes sharply. Without guidance, this is easily mistaken for progress.

It is not.

Insight without regulation borrows energy from stability. It feels expansive before it feels exhausting.

By the time collapse becomes visible, the window for gentle integration has often closed.

This is why ancient traditions surrounded insight with safeguards.

Not because insight was dangerous — but because uncontained insight is.

Silence, routine, service, ethical discipline, and community were not moral requirements. They were stabilizing structures.

Modern systems removed the symbolism without replacing the scaffolding.

The tragedy is that many individuals now encounter this edge alone.

They are told either:

- "This means nothing — ignore it," or
- "This means everything — follow it completely"

Both responses are destabilizing.

What is needed instead is something quieter:

To recognize insight as a **phase**, not an identity.
To treat regulation as essential, not optional.
To prioritize emotional safety over interpretation.

This distinction matters because it determines what follows.

Some individuals return from insight calmer, clearer, and more compassionate. Others return anxious, brittle, or fragmented — not because they saw too much, but because they were not supported in *how* to see.

Understanding this difference is not spiritual knowledge.

It is psychological literacy.

Where Responsibility Begins

This chapter marks an important boundary.

Faith often celebrated insight without responsibility. Science often prioritized stability without transformation.

The path forward requires both.

To recognize insight as humanly possible — and integration as non-negotiable.

That recognition prepares us for the next step: understanding how emotions like love, trust, fear, and hatred shape not just individuals, but entire societies.

Chapter 5
Love, Trust, Fear — Emotional Technologies of Transformation

Human beings are not governed primarily by reason. They are governed by emotion.

Reason explains *after* emotion decides.

This has been true since the earliest human communities, and it remains true in modern societies shaped by media, politics, and institutions. The most powerful forces shaping human behavior are not ideas or beliefs—but emotional states that operate beneath them.

Religious traditions understood this long before psychology named it.

Emotion as a Regulatory Force

Emotion is not the opposite of intelligence. It is a **regulatory signal**.

Fear narrows attention.
Trust widens it.
Love stabilizes it.
Hatred distorts it.

Neuroscience now confirms that emotional states directly affect perception, memory, and decision-making. A fearful mind sees threat where none exists. A trusting mind tolerates ambiguity. A loving mind remains open even under pressure.

Religious teachings focused on emotion not because they were sentimental—but because **emotion determines behavior more reliably than instruction**.

Why Love Was Central

Love appears so frequently in religious teaching that it is often dismissed as idealism.

It is not.

Love reduces defensive arousal in the nervous system. When fear subsides, cognitive flexibility increases. This allows curiosity, empathy, and learning to emerge. In practical terms, love disarms hostility more effectively than force.

This is why teachings emphasized love of neighbor, compassion for the weak, forgiveness of enemies—not as moral commands, but as **methods of transformation**.

You cannot reason a fearful person into clarity. You must first make them feel safe.

▢ Teachings on Love

- **Christianity:** "Love your neighbor as yourself."
- **Islam:** "None of you truly believes until he loves for his brother what he loves for himself."
- **Hinduism:** *Ahimsa* (non-violence)
- **Buddhism:** *Metta* (loving-kindness)
- **Sikhism:** Compassion (*Daya*) as divine quality

Trust as the Foundation of Influence

Trust is the emotion that allows surrender without fear.

Where trust exists, people listen. Where it does not, control must replace influence. This is why religious figures who inspired trust could move societies without armies or institutions.

Trust emerges when words, actions, and inner state align.

This alignment was sensed instinctively. People did not follow because they were convinced—but because they *felt safe* in the presence of clarity.

Modern leadership studies echo this truth, though often in diluted form.

Fear as a Tool — and a Trap

Fear is the most efficient short-term motivator.

It produces obedience, conformity, and rapid coordination. This is why fear has been repeatedly exploited by religious institutions, political systems, and social hierarchies.

But fear carries a cost.

It fragments perception, reduces empathy, and creates enemies where none existed. Sustained fear erodes trust and eventually destabilizes the very systems that rely on it.

Religious teachings warned against fear-based control not because it was immoral—but because it was **unsustainable**.

☐ Teachings on Fear

- **Christianity:** "Perfect love casts out fear."
- **Islam:** Fear of God balanced with mercy
- **Hinduism:** Fear arising from ignorance (*Avidya*)
- **Buddhism:** Fear as attachment to impermanence
- **Sikhism:** Fear dissolves through remembrance (*Naam*)

How These Emotions Shape Everyday Life

Fear and Care Inside Families

Fear most often enters human life wearing the face of care.

In families, fear rarely appears as threat or aggression. It appears as concern, protection, and responsibility. A parent controls because they are afraid of loss. They restrict because they are afraid of harm. They intervene because uncertainty feels intolerable.

From the inside, this does not feel like fear.
It feels like love doing its duty.

Yet children do not respond primarily to intention. They respond to emotional atmosphere.

A home regulated by fear teaches vigilance. A home regulated by trust teaches resilience. In both cases, the lesson is absorbed long before it is understood.

Many adults carry emotional reflexes formed in childhood without ever questioning them.

They anticipate criticism before it arrives.
They equate closeness with control.
They associate safety with obedience.

These patterns persist not because parents failed, but because fear was inherited without awareness. Religion once tried to soften this inheritance by emphasizing compassion, forgiveness, and mercy — not as virtues, but as interruptions to fear transmission.

Modern psychology now recognizes the same mechanism under different language.

What makes this difficult is that fear-based care often *works* in the short term.

Children comply. Order is maintained. Risk is reduced. But the cost appears later — in diminished confidence, anxiety, or dependence on external approval.

Love without trust becomes suffocating.
Care without allowance for error becomes control.

This is not a moral failure. It is an emotional one.

When families begin to examine emotion rather than behavior, something shifts.

The question changes from:
"How do I make this stop?"
to:
"What am I afraid will happen if I don't intervene?"

That single shift introduces awareness — and awareness alters emotional transmission.

This is the smallest scale at which emotional regulation reshapes the future.

In workplaces and systems of authority, emotion rarely announces itself openly.

Fear is framed as accountability.
Control is framed as efficiency.
Distrust is framed as professionalism.

Unlike families, where emotional tone is felt directly, institutional environments mask emotion behind process, policy, and performance metrics. Yet the underlying forces are the same.

A culture shaped by fear produces compliance, caution, and exhaustion. A culture shaped by trust produces ownership, learning, and resilience. The difference is not structural — it is emotional.

Trust, Fear, and Control in Workplaces and Authority

In workplaces and systems of authority, emotion rarely appears in its raw form.

Fear does not look like panic.
Distrust does not look like hostility.
Control does not look like aggression.

They are reframed as professionalism, accountability, and efficiency.

This is why emotional climates in organizations are often misread as cultural issues or leadership styles, when they are in fact **regulatory states**.

Fear-driven workplaces are usually described as "high-performing."

Deadlines are tight. Metrics are visible. Oversight is constant. People respond quickly — but cautiously. Innovation narrows. Mistakes are hidden. Learning slows.

From the inside, this feels like responsibility.

From the nervous system's perspective, it is vigilance.

People in such environments spend more energy managing perception than solving problems. Trust is replaced by surveillance, and motivation is sustained through pressure rather than ownership.

Trust-driven workplaces feel slower at first.

They tolerate ambiguity.
They allow errors to surface.
They distribute responsibility rather than centralizing control.

This can appear inefficient to those accustomed to fear-based urgency. But over time, such environments outperform because attention is not consumed by self-protection.

People think more clearly when they are not being watched for failure.

This is not a cultural preference.
It is a biological reality.

Leadership amplifies these emotional patterns.

Leaders who operate from unresolved fear often rely on control — not because they are authoritarian by nature, but because uncertainty feels dangerous. They tighten processes, demand alignment, and mistake compliance for commitment.

Leaders grounded in trust behave differently. They listen without defensiveness. They tolerate disagreement. They allow others to carry uncertainty without punishing it.

The difference is not charisma or strategy.
It is emotional regulation.

Modern organizations struggle here because emotion is treated as noise rather than signal.

Performance frameworks measure output but ignore the emotional cost of sustaining it. Burnout is treated as individual weakness rather than systemic dysregulation.

Religion once attempted to humanize authority by emphasizing humility and service. Modern management literature gestures toward the same ideas, but often without addressing the emotional foundation that makes them possible.

What makes workplaces especially powerful is that they **recondition adults**.

Long after childhood patterns are set, organizational environments reinforce fear or trust daily. Over time, people internalize these emotional climates, carrying them back into families, relationships, and public life.

This is how emotional technologies scale.

Understanding this prepares us for a more uncomfortable truth:

Systems do not become controlling by accident.
They become controlling when fear is institutionalized.

And that is the thread we must now follow.

Love, Fear, and Public Narratives

What families transmit privately, societies amplify publicly.

Fear scales faster than trust because it requires less stability. It spreads through images, headlines, and repetition. It simplifies complexity into threat and identity into opposition.

Public narratives rarely persuade through reason. They mobilize through emotion.

This is not manipulation alone. It is emotional physics.

Love, by contrast, does not scale through language easily.

It requires embodiment — consistency, restraint, and visible care without performance. This makes it slow, fragile, and difficult to broadcast. As a result, public discourse defaults toward fear even when collective desire leans toward cooperation.

Religion once attempted to stabilize this imbalance by ritualizing compassion and limiting retaliation. Modern systems attempt to regulate it through policy and law. Neither succeeds without emotional literacy.

Moral outrage is one of fear's most effective disguises.

It feels righteous, energizing, and purposeful. It offers belonging without vulnerability. Yet it often amplifies the very conditions it claims to oppose.

People become attached not to resolution, but to emotional activation.

Love does not offer this reward.
Trust does not feel urgent.
Fear does.

This is why societies repeatedly cycle through division even when progress is possible.

Emotional regulation has not scaled with technological reach. The tools of amplification outpaced the maturity of emotional awareness.

Religion sensed this danger early. Science now measures its effects. Neither alone has solved it.

The implication is uncomfortable but necessary:

Until emotion is understood as a **primary driver**, systems will continue to misdiagnose moral failure where emotional dysregulation is the root.

This recognition does not excuse harm.
It explains persistence.

The uncomfortable truth is that **emotion precedes values**.

People rarely act against what they feel, no matter what they claim to believe. This is why moral instruction fails without emotional regulation, and why systems built on fear eventually collapse under their own rigidity.

Religion spoke in moral language.
Psychology speaks in emotional language.

They are pointing to the same mechanism.

How Emotion Scales from Individuals to Societies

Emotion does not stop at the individual.

Groups amplify emotion. Shared fear becomes collective paranoia. Shared trust becomes cohesion. Shared resentment becomes ideology. Shared love becomes movement.

This is why prophets addressed crowds, not just individuals. They were regulating **collective emotional states**.

When love and trust dominated, societies stabilized. When fear and hatred took over, collapse followed—often disguised as righteousness.

History repeats this pattern relentlessly.

When Emotional Strategy Becomes Governance

In unstable eras, leaders quickly recognize what modern psychology now confirms: emotion is the fastest lever of collective behavior.

Ancient political thinkers such as Chanakya understood this deeply. In times of fragmentation and external threat, governance required not only administration but emotional management. Fear consolidated loyalty. External enemies unified divided populations. Division clarified identity. Suspicion preserved power.

These were not necessarily acts of cruelty. They were survival strategies for volatile environments.

But survival intelligence has a limit.

What stabilizes a fractured society through fear cannot sustainably govern a mature one. Fear demands constant renewal. It requires new threats, new divisions, new emotional triggers. Over time, the system becomes dependent on emotional volatility to maintain cohesion.

And volatility erodes trust.

This is the silent turning point in civilizations. Power may remain intact. Institutions may continue functioning. But emotional fatigue begins to spread beneath the surface. Cohesion weakens even when authority appears strong.

When governance relies primarily on amplified emotion rather than regulated emotion, collapse does not begin with rebellion. It begins with quiet disengagement.

This is why fear-based systems eventually become brittle. They mistake emotional activation for stability.

Clarity-Based Cohesion

If emotion precedes values, then emotional maturity must precede stable systems.

Clarity-based cohesion does not deny emotion. It regulates it. It does not suppress fear; it understands its origin. It does not manufacture enemies; it reduces projection. It does not depend on division to maintain identity; it builds identity through shared meaning.

Where fear-based governance accelerates reaction, clarity-based influence slows perception.
Where manipulation amplifies insecurity, clarity diffuses it.
Where emotional volatility creates urgency, emotional literacy creates steadiness.

This shift is subtle but decisive.

When individuals understand their emotional drivers, collective manipulation loses effectiveness. Division becomes harder to engineer. Polarization loses velocity. Cohesion begins to emerge not from shared threat but from shared understanding.

Religion attempted this through moral frameworks. Psychology attempts it through emotional awareness. Both recognize the same truth: without regulation of emotion, no value system can hold.

The evolution required now is not technological. It is emotional.

Until emotional regulation scales with influence, societies will continue cycling through fear and fragmentation—even while believing themselves to be progressing.

Why Power Corrupts Emotional Balance

Power multiplies emotional consequence.

Leaders operating from fear project fear outward. Leaders grounded in trust distribute stability. This is why religious traditions placed such emphasis on humility, restraint, and service in positions of authority.

Power without inner clarity amplifies unresolved emotion. Clarity without power remains limited in reach.

Balancing the two has always been humanity's central challenge.

What makes this difficult is that emotional patterns feel personal.

To notice fear feels like failure.
To acknowledge distrust feels disloyal.
To examine love feels vulnerable.

So, most people avoid looking directly.

Yet without this examination, emotion continues to shape behavior invisibly — and power exploits what remains unconscious.

This is why emotion was always the quiet battleground beneath belief.

Understanding this prepares us to see how systems learned to use emotion deliberately — not to liberate, but to organize, control, and preserve themselves.

And that is where we turn next.

What This Means for the Individual

Emotion is not something to suppress or transcend.

It is something to **understand and regulate**.

When individuals learn to observe their own fear, cultivate trust, and stabilize love, their influence changes naturally. They stop needing control. Their presence becomes sufficient.

This is not idealism. It is observable reality.

▢ Emotional Discipline in Leadership

- **Christianity:** Servant leadership
- **Islam:** Accountability before God
- **Hinduism:** *Raja Dharma* (duty of rulers)
- **Buddhism:** Right intention
- **Sikhism:** Leadership through service (*Seva*)

The Uncomfortable Truth

Religious systems failed not because they spoke of love—but because they taught it as instruction rather than cultivation.

Emotion cannot be commanded.
It must be experienced, regulated, and integrated.

Understanding this distinction prepares us to examine where religion diverged most sharply from its original intent: when lived experience hardened into system and structure.

That is where we turn next.

Chapter 6
When Living Truth Hardened into Organized Power

Living truth does not require protection.
Power does.

The moment a teaching begins to influence large numbers of people; a subtle shift occurs. What was once lived becomes guarded. What was once shared becomes regulated. What was once fluid becomes fixed.

This is not a failure of religion alone.
It is a predictable pattern of human systems.

Why Organization Was Inevitable

As communities grew, shared meaning needed structure.

Stories had to be preserved. Practices had to be standardized. Authority had to be defined. Without organization, teachings fragmented or disappeared entirely.

This was not corruption at first. It was preservation.

Rules emerged to maintain coherence. Hierarchies formed to ensure continuity. Symbols became markers of identity. Over time, what began as guidance became governance.

Religion did not begin as control.
It became control when scale demanded certainty.

The Shift from Experience to Authority

The original teachers spoke from direct experience. Their authority came from clarity, not position. But experience cannot be inherited. Authority can.

As generations passed, institutions formed to *represent* the teaching. Over time, representation replaced realization.

This created a structural inversion:

- Obedience replaced understanding.
- Belief replaced inquiry.
- Identity replaced integration.

Once authority detached from lived insight, power entered the system.

☐ Institutionalization Across Traditions

- **Christianity:** Church hierarchy and doctrinal councils
- **Islam:** Caliphates and schools of jurisprudence
- **Hinduism:** Caste stratification and ritual authority
- **Buddhism:** Monastic hierarchies and doctrinal schools
- **Sikhism:** Codification of scripture and discipline

Fear as the Simplest Tool

Power must maintain compliance.

The most efficient way to do so is fear—fear of punishment, fear of exclusion, fear of divine consequence. Fear simplifies decision-making and discourages questioning.

This is where symbolic language hardened into literal threat.

Heaven and hell became destinations instead of states. Sin became crime instead of misalignment. Doubt became betrayal instead of inquiry.

Fear-based control is effective in the short term. It is corrosive in the long term.

▢ Fear and Control in Religious Language

- **Christianity:** Eternal damnation
- **Islam:** Fear of judgment without balance of mercy
- **Hinduism:** Fear of karmic punishment without context
- **Buddhism:** Fear-based interpretations of rebirth
- **Sikhism:** Ritual compliance over inner remembrance

Identity as a Substitute for Insight

Once fear enters, identity follows.

Belief becomes a badge. Membership becomes protection. Outsiders become threats. What was meant to dissolve ego becomes fuel for it.

Religion shifts from inner work to group allegiance.

This is not unique to faith. Political ideologies, national identities, and even scientific dogma follow the same pattern when certainty replaces curiosity.

Identity offers belonging without responsibility.

When Distortion Begins Before Belief

Identity hardens when perception is already distorted. Faith traditions across cultures often focused on regulating behavior—what one should see, hear, or say. These prescriptions were not arbitrary. They arose from an intuitive understanding that distorted inputs reinforce inner disorder. When Mahatma Gandhi spoke of *not seeing, hearing, or speaking evil*, it is commonly read as a moral directive. More accurately, it was a pragmatic restraint—an attempt to prevent further contamination of an already unsettled mind.

Yet restraint addresses the symptom, not the source.

Distortion does not begin at the level of the senses. The eyes and ears largely report what is present. The corruption enters through interpretation—through thought shaped by fear, resentment, prejudice, or inherited assumptions. When these filters remain unexamined, perception itself becomes unreliable. What one "sees" in the world is no longer reality, but reflection.

This distinction becomes clearer when viewed beyond religious contexts.

Nelson Mandela, after decades of imprisonment, emerged without bitterness toward his oppressors. This was not moral idealism. It was perceptual clarity. Mandela understood that resentment would distort judgment, narrow possibility, and quietly perpetuate the very violence he sought to end. By refusing to let inner narratives of hatred define what he saw in others, he preserved the accuracy of perception required to build a future rather than repeat the past.

Modern psychology articulates this mechanism even more explicitly. Carl Jung observed that what remains unconscious does not disappear—it projects itself outward. Individuals then experience their own unresolved inner content as hostility, threat, or fate imposed by the world. In such cases, belief systems become convenient justifications for distortion rather than paths to clarity. One does not merely believe wrongly; one *perceives wrongly* and then defends that perception as truth.

This is where faith, over time, became misunderstood.

Instead of guiding individuals toward examining the quality of their thoughts, traditions increasingly emphasized control of behavior and belief. Moral discipline replaced cognitive inquiry. Obedience replaced understanding. What began as an attempt to restore perceptual alignment hardened into systems that managed conduct while leaving distortion intact.

True clarity does not require constant restraint. When thought is examined and aligned, perception corrects itself. One no longer needs to avoid evil deliberately; misinterpretation fails to arise. In that sense, faith was never meant to suppress human experience—it was meant to clean the lens through which experience is seen.

What was lost was not faith itself, but insight into where distortion truly begins.

Once belief begins protecting distortion rather than dissolving it, any attempt at clarity feels like a threat.

Why Reformers Were Resisted

Every tradition produced individuals who attempted to restore original clarity. They emphasized experience over doctrine, compassion over control, and inquiry over obedience.

They were rarely welcomed.

Systems resist disruption not because reformers are wrong—but because clarity threatens dependency.

▢Reformers and Resistance

- **Christianity:** Early mystics and reformers
- **Islam:** Sufi traditions
- **Hinduism:** Bhakti movement
- **Buddhism:** Zen and reform schools
- **Sikhism:** Emphasis on lived discipline over ritual.

The Cost of Organized Power

When power override's purpose, three things follow:

1. Teachings become rigid.
2. Leaders become gatekeepers.

3. Followers become dependent.

Faith shifts from inner alignment to external compliance.

Ironically, the very structures meant to preserve wisdom begin to obstruct it.

What Survived Despite the System

Yet something endured.

Even within rigid systems, individuals continued to experience clarity, compassion, and transformation. The inner truth proved more resilient than the structures around it.

This suggests something important:

Truth does not belong to institutions.
Institutions only attempt to contain it.

How Power Preserves Itself

Organized power does not begin with corruption.

It begins with coordination.

Whenever human activity scales beyond small groups, structure becomes necessary. Roles are defined. Rules are formalized. Authority is assigned. Without this, collective effort collapses into chaos.

This is how institutions are born.

The problem does not arise from organization itself, but from what happens after stability is achieved.

From Guidance to Governance

In the early stages, authority serves understanding.

Leaders explain. Elders guide. Experts contextualize. The system remains porous, responsive to lived reality.

Over time, a subtle inversion occurs.

Authority shifts from explaining meaning to enforcing compliance. Guidance hardens into governance. What was once provisional becomes final.

This shift rarely feels oppressive from the inside. It feels efficient.

Questions slow things down. Experience introduces variability. Certainty simplifies coordination. So, systems gradually reward obedience over insight—not because insight is wrong, but because it is unpredictable.

Religion was simply the earliest arena where this played out at scale.

Modern Institutions, Ancient Patterns

What happened to religion did not end with religion.

Corporations, governments, academic bodies, and even scientific institutions now exhibit the same dynamics. Policies replace judgment. Metrics replace meaning. Procedure replaces responsibility.

Individuals are evaluated by adherence rather than understanding.

This creates systems that appear rational but feel hollow. People comply without conviction. Innovation becomes risky. Dissent is framed as disruption rather than contribution.

Power stabilizes itself by narrowing acceptable behavior.

The language changes. The pattern does not.

When Fear Becomes Structural

The most reliable way for power to preserve itself is to institutionalize fear.

Not overt fear—subtle fear.

Fear of exclusion.
Fear of failure.
Fear of reputational loss.
Fear of being misaligned with the dominant narrative.

Once fear is structural, individuals police themselves. Authority no longer needs to coerce. Compliance becomes voluntary.

This is why reform is so difficult.

Those who question the system are not silenced through force. They are marginalized through process.

Religion once used salvation and damnation.
Modern systems use performance reviews, funding decisions, and social credibility.

The mechanism is identical.

Organized power does not require malice to function this way.

It requires only one thing: the avoidance of uncertainty.

Clarity introduces unpredictability.
Experience resists standardization.
Awareness cannot be fully controlled.

So, systems prefer rule-followers to clear thinkers.

The tragedy is that systems forget their original purpose.

What was meant to serve human flourishing begins to demand loyalty. What was meant to preserve truth begins to defend itself. Reformers are tolerated only until they threaten stability.

This is why every major tradition—and every modern institution—eventually resists the very insight that gave it life.

Why This Matters Now

Modern societies face the same challenge under different names.

Corporations, governments, media, and even scientific institutions struggle with the same tension: preserving order without suppressing truth.

Religion was simply the earliest large-scale experiment.

Understanding this does not require rejection. It requires discernment.

Where the Divide Deepens

Once religion became system, science began its rise—initially as rebellion, later as alternative authority. But science, too, would inherit the same temptations of power.

The next chapter explores this divergence—and why neither path alone was sufficient.

Chapter 7
Faith, Science, And The Great Divide

The divide between faith and science did not arise from disagreement about truth.
It arose from disagreement about **authority**.

Both were seeking understanding.
Both were reacting to distortion.
And both, in different ways, overcorrected.

When Inquiry Became Dangerous

As religious institutions consolidated power, inquiry became a threat.

Questions destabilized certainty. Experience challenged doctrine. Observation undermined interpretation. Over time, curiosity was reframed as doubt—and doubt as disobedience.

This was not because faith feared truth.
It was because **power fears unpredictability**.

When authority depends on fixed answers, open inquiry becomes intolerable.

☐ **Suppression of Inquiry**

- **Christianity:** Heresy trials and doctrinal enforcement
- **Islam:** Closure of certain interpretive traditions
- **Hinduism:** Ritual orthodoxy overshadowing inquiry.
- **Buddhism:** Institutional resistance to reform movements
- **Sikhism:** Tension between discipline and inner realization

---

Science as a Necessary Rebellion

Science emerged not to deny meaning—but to reclaim **freedom of inquiry**.

Observation replaced obedience.
Evidence replaced authority.
Repeatability replaced revelation.

This shift was essential.

The external world needed to be understood without fear of punishment. Nature needed to be observed as it was, not as doctrine demanded it to be.

Science succeeded precisely because it refused to answer questions it could not test.

The Cost of That Success

But in rejecting untestable claims, science gradually distanced itself from inner experience.

Consciousness became a by-product.
Emotion became chemistry.
Meaning became subjective—and therefore irrelevant.

What could not be measured was sidelined, not because it was false, but because it was inconvenient.

This created a new imbalance.

Religion claimed inner truth without verification.
Science claimed external truth without meaning.

Both were incomplete.

▢ Diverging Priorities

- **Religion:** Meaning, morality, inner life
- **Science:** Measurement, prediction, control
- **Conflict Point:** Authority over explanation
- **Blind Spots:** Literalism vs reductionism

Why the Divide Persisted

The divide endured because each side defined itself in opposition to the other.

Religion saw science as a threat to meaning.
Science saw religion as an obstacle to progress.

Neither noticed that they were addressing **different dimensions of the same human experience**.

Faith was concerned with *how humans live.*
Science was concerned with *how reality behaves.*

The tragedy was not disagreement—it was isolation.

The Unspoken Agreement

There was also a quieter reason for the divide.

Both systems benefited from separation.

Religion retained moral authority by avoiding scrutiny. Science retained credibility by avoiding subjectivity.

Each protected its domain by refusing integration.

▢ Mutual Avoidance

- **Religion:** "Science cannot explain the soul."
- **Science:** "Religion is untestable."
- **Result:** Fragmented understanding of the human condition

---

The Cracks Begin to Show

In recent decades, this separation has become increasingly strained.

Psychology confronts emotion and belief.
Neuroscience studies consciousness.

Medicine recognizes placebo and stress effects.
Physics questions the observer's role.

Science is circling back toward questions faith never stopped asking—without adopting faith's language.

This is not convergence.
It is *rediscovery*.

Why Integration Is Now Unavoidable

Modern humans live in both worlds simultaneously.

They rely on science for survival.
They rely on meaning for sanity.

Ignoring either creates imbalance.

The question is no longer whether faith and science can coexist.
It is whether humanity can afford their continued separation.

What This Book Is Not Attempting

This book does not seek to spiritualize science or scientize faith.

It seeks to **translate**.

To recognize that ancient teachings described inner realities symbolically, while modern science describes external realities precisely—and that both are observing the same human system from different angles.

Where This Leaves the Reader

If faith misunderstood meaning, and science misunderstood experience, then clarity lies elsewhere.

Not in belief.
Not in denial.
But in **integration**.

That integration requires revisiting symbols, not as facts—but as **maps**.

That is where we turn next.

Chapter 8
How Symbols Replaced Understanding

Symbols were never meant to be believed.
They were meant to be *understood.*

Every spiritual tradition relied on symbols because symbols do something language cannot: they point beyond themselves. They compress complex inner realities into forms that can be remembered, shared, and transmitted across generations.

The problem did not begin with symbols.
It began when symbols were mistaken for facts.

Why Symbols Were Necessary

Human inner experience is subtle.

Emotions shift faster than words. Awareness cannot be captured directly. Insight often arrives as sensation, not statement. Early teachers faced a fundamental limitation: how to communicate experiences that listeners had not yet lived.

Symbols solved this problem.

A story could carry meaning without explanation.
A metaphor could survive translation.
A ritual could transmit state, not concept.

Symbols were **bridges**, not conclusions.

When Meaning Detached from Experience

As teachings spread, fewer people had direct access to the experiences behind the symbols.

Stories were repeated by those who had not lived them. Rituals were performed without understanding their regulatory function. Over time, *familiarity replaced insight.*

What was once symbolic became literal.

Heaven became a place.
Hell became a threat.
God became an external authority.
Salvation became a transaction.

The symbol remained—but its purpose was forgotten.

▢ Symbol to Literal Across Traditions

- **Christianity:** Resurrection as afterlife event rather than inner renewal
- **Islam:** Judgment day imagery read as future spectacle.
- **Hinduism:** Deities read as historical beings rather than archetypal forces.
- **Buddhism:** Rebirth read as metaphysical claim rather than continuity of conditioning.
- **Sikhism:** Ritual identity overtaking inner remembrance.

Why Literalism Feels Safer

Literal belief offers certainty.

It removes ambiguity.
It simplifies responsibility.
It creates clear rules and consequences.

Understanding, by contrast, demands effort and self-examination. It requires the individual to confront their own fear, ego, and inconsistency.

For large populations, certainty scales better than clarity.

This is why institutions favor literalism—not out of malice, but out of necessity.

The Hidden Cost of Literalism

When symbols harden into facts, several things happen simultaneously:

- Inner inquiry slows.
- Fear becomes enforceable.
- Authority consolidates.
- Doubt becomes dangerous.

Most critically, personal responsibility diminishes.

If salvation is external, inner work becomes optional.
If punishment is deferred, behavior becomes performative.
If meaning is prescribed, awareness atrophies.

Religion survives—but wisdom thins.

Why Science Reacted So Strongly

Science rejected literal religious claims not because symbolism was false, but because literalism made claims about the external world that failed verification.

In doing so, science threw out the symbol along with the superstition.

What was lost was not belief—but **inner literacy**.

Symbols were dismissed as primitive instead of translated. Subjective experience was sidelined instead of studied.

This left modern humans with extraordinary control over matter—but limited understanding of meaning.

▢ Modern Parallels of Literalism

- **Ideologies:** Slogans replacing thought
- **Politics:** Identity replacing policy
- **Science:** Metrics replacing lived experience
- **Technology:** Engagement replacing understanding

The mechanism is the same. Only the symbols change.

The Quiet Failure of Both Sides

Religion preserved symbols without inquiry.
Science pursued inquiry without symbols.

One guarded meaning but resisted questioning.
The other mastered questioning but avoided meaning.

The result is a world rich in explanation and poor in wisdom.

What Survived Beneath the Symbol

Despite distortion, symbols never fully lost their power.

People still feel peace in prayer.
Still experience clarity in silence.
Still find transformation in service.

This is because symbols work **even when misunderstood**, as long as the underlying human system remains the same.

The danger is not that symbols fail.
The danger is that people stop learning *why* they work.

Where Literalism Reappears Today

The collapse of symbolic understanding did not end with religion.

It migrated.

When religious symbols lost authority, the human need for certainty did not disappear. It found new containers — modern, rational, and socially sanctioned.

Literalism did not retreat.
It changed language.

Metrics Replacing Meaning

Modern systems increasingly rely on measurement to determine value.

Performance is tracked. Productivity is quantified.
Engagement is counted. Progress is graphed.

These tools are not inherently flawed. They are symbolic representations of complex realities. The problem begins when the symbol replaces the reality it was meant to indicate.

When numbers become goals rather than references, behavior warps. People optimize for metrics instead of meaning. Teaching becomes test preparation. Healthcare becomes throughput. Work becomes output detached from purpose.

This is not rationality.
It is literalism wearing empirical clothing.

Identity Labels as Modern Symbols

Identity labels were once descriptors. They are now treated as essence.

Psychological categories, social identities, political affiliations, and even personality frameworks are increasingly used to define people rather than understand them.

What began as symbolic shorthand hardens into fixed identity. Complexity is flattened. Growth becomes betrayal. Disagreement becomes threat.

Religion once mistook symbolic roles for eternal truth. Modern culture repeats the pattern by mistaking labels for lived reality.

The symbol survives.
Understanding does not.

Productivity, Optimization, and the New Rituals

Ritual did not disappear with faith.

It became optimization.

Morning routines, productivity systems, performance hacks, and self-improvement doctrines now promise control over uncertainty. They offer structure, predictability, and reassurance — often without addressing underlying meaning.

Like religious rituals before them, these practices work *until they are mistaken for the goal.*

When optimization replaces understanding, burnout follows. The ritual remains, but its purpose is forgotten.

This is not progress away from symbolism.
It is symbolism stripped of reflection.

Modern literalism feels safer because it appears objective.

Numbers do not argue. Labels do not hesitate. Systems do not ask uncomfortable questions.

But objectivity without interpretation becomes blind.

The cost is subtle but cumulative.

Meaning erodes quietly. People perform rather than participate. Success is achieved without satisfaction. Systems function while individuals fragment.

This is the same hollowing that occurred when religious symbols hardened into doctrine.

Only the vocabulary has changed.

Recovering Meaning Without Regression

Reclaiming symbolic understanding does not require returning to belief.

It requires learning to read symbols as **maps of inner states**, not as descriptions of external reality.

This restores agency.

The question shifts from:
"What must I believe?"
to:
"What is this pointing to within me?"

That shift is the beginning of maturity.

Where This Leads Next

Once symbols are recognized as maps, a deeper layer becomes visible—one religion could never fully articulate on its own:

That belief itself alters perception, biology, and outcome.

This is where modern science quietly reconnects with ancient intuition.

Interlude I
One Insight, Many Languages

The Insight: Fear Contracts, Awareness Liberates

Every major tradition recognized a central psychological truth:

Human suffering intensifies when fear dominates perception, and diminishes when awareness stabilizes attention.

This insight did not emerge from philosophy alone. It emerged from lived observation — of individuals, communities, and leaders.

What follows is not comparison for equivalence, but **parallel pointing**.

Christianity

Love, Fear, and Inner Orientation

Christian teachings repeatedly emphasize love not as sentiment, but as orientation.

"Perfect love casts out fear" was not a moral command. It was an observation: when fear loosens, behavior reorganizes naturally. Forgiveness becomes possible. Compassion emerges without effort.

The "Kingdom of God" was not consistently described as a future location, but as a present state — *within.* Parables were used precisely because direct explanation failed to transmit inner shifts.

Early Christian mystics understood this clearly. Later institutional Christianity struggled to preserve the insight without turning it into belief.

Islam

Submission as Inner Alignment

At its core, Islam emphasizes *tawhid* — unity — not merely of God, but of orientation.

Submission (*Islam*) was never intended as obedience to authority alone. It described the reduction of inner conflict: aligning intention, action, and awareness toward coherence rather than fear.

Fear (*khauf*) was acknowledged, but always balanced with mercy (*rahma*). Without this balance, submission degenerates into compliance — a distortion many later systems inherited.

Sufi traditions preserved the experiential core long after formal structures hardened.

Hinduism

Ignorance, Fear, and Misidentification

Hindu philosophical traditions approached suffering through misidentification.

Avidya (ignorance) did not mean lack of information. It meant mistaking transient states — body, thought, emotion — for identity.

Fear arose naturally from this misidentification. Liberation (*moksha*) was not escape from the world, but release from compulsive attachment to limited self-concepts.

Stories of gods, demons, and cosmic battles were symbolic maps of inner dynamics — not historical claims.

Buddhism

Suffering as a Cognitive Pattern

Buddhism made one of the most precise psychological claims of any tradition:

Suffering arises from attachment, not circumstance.

Fear was understood as a response to impermanence. The mind resists change, clings to stability, and generates distress when reality refuses to comply.

Mindfulness was not spiritual practice, but **attention training** — learning to observe without identification.

Where later traditions spoke symbolically, Buddhism spoke clinically.

Sikhism

Fearlessness Through Remembrance

Sikh teachings placed fearlessness (*nirbhau*) at the center of human dignity.

This was not bravado or resistance, but inner steadiness arising from remembrance (*Naam*). When attention stabilizes, fear loses its grip.

Sikhism resisted withdrawal from the world. Integration happened through family life, work, and service — an insistence that clarity must survive ordinary conditions.

This made it one of the most psychologically grounded traditions.

What Is Striking — and What Is Not

What is striking is not that these traditions used different metaphors.

What is striking is that:

- Fear is universally recognized as distortive
- Awareness is universally stabilizing
- Compassion emerges naturally from clarity
- Identity hardens when fear dominates

What is *not* striking is how often these insights were later institutionalized, ritualized, and defended — losing the very flexibility they were meant to cultivate.

Chapter 9
Faith, Gratitude, And Collective Memory

Not all memory is personal.

Some memories shape individuals.
Others shape families, communities, and entire cultures—long after the original experience has passed.

Religious traditions intuited this long before science could observe it. What they described as blessing, curse, grace, or inheritance was an attempt to explain a simple but profound truth:

Experience does not end with the individual.

Memory Beyond the Individual

Modern neuroscience recognizes that memory is not only stored as conscious recollection. It is embedded in emotional responses, stress patterns, expectations, and behavior.

A child can inherit fear without knowing its origin.
A community can inherit resilience without remembering its source.

What persists is not the event—but its *emotional residue.*

Religious language preserved this insight symbolically, because there was no other way to transmit it.

Gratitude as a Stabilizing Force

Gratitude appears repeatedly across traditions, often framed as devotion, prayer, or remembrance.

This is not moral advice.
It is emotional regulation.

Gratitude shifts attention away from threat and scarcity toward safety and continuity. It calms the nervous system. It stabilizes perception. Communities anchored in gratitude recover faster from disruption than those anchored in grievance.

This is why gratitude became ritualized.

Not to please a deity—but to **protect collective stability**.

☐ Teachings on Gratitude

- **Christianity:** Giving thanks in all circumstances
- **Islam:** *Shukr* (gratitude) as a sign of faith
- **Hinduism:** Gratitude toward ancestors and nature
- **Buddhism:** Appreciation (*Mudita*) and mindfulness
- **Sikhism:** Gratitude through remembrance (*Naam*)

Trauma, Memory, and Inheritance

Just as gratitude stabilizes, unresolved trauma destabilizes.

Communities that endure displacement, violence, famine, or persecution often carry heightened vigilance across generations. Even when circumstances improve, the body remembers.

Science now observes this through epigenetics: changes in gene expression influenced by stress and safety—not by altering DNA, but by regulating how genes are activated.

Religious narratives of ancestral burden were early attempts to articulate this continuity.

They were not claims of punishment.
They were warnings about **unintegrated experience**.

Why Faith Preserved Memory Symbolically

Collective memory cannot be stored as data. It must be *felt* to endure.

Stories, rituals, commemorations, and moral codes ensured that emotionally significant experiences were not forgotten—even when their original context faded.

Faith functioned as a **memory scaffold**.

It held lessons in place until humanity developed the tools to examine them consciously.

▢ Ancestral Continuity in Texts

- **Christianity:** Generational blessing and consequence
- **Islam:** Accountability across lineage
- **Hinduism:** *Pitru Paksha* and ancestral remembrance
- **Buddhism:** Continuity of conditioning
- **Sikhism:** Lineage refined through awareness, not fear

When Memory Turns into Identity

There is a risk embedded here.

When collective memory is not examined, it hardens into identity. Gratitude becomes entitlement. Trauma becomes grievance. History becomes justification.

Religion struggled here because memory was preserved without tools for reinterpretation.

What was meant to be remembered became something to defend.

The Quiet Biological Confirmation

Science has not "proven" religious ideas—but it has confirmed their **direction**.

Experience leaves traces.
Emotion outlives events.
Meaning shapes behavior long after explanation fades.

The language has changed. The mechanism has not.

How Memory Lives Beyond Experience

Collective memory does not announce itself as history.

It appears as reflex.

A hesitation where none is required.
A loyalty that feels instinctive.
A fear that seems disproportionate to the present moment.

People often attribute these reactions to personality, culture, or temperament. Rarely do they recognize them as unfinished memory.

Families as Memory Carriers

Families are the smallest units of collective memory.

Long before stories are told, emotional tone is transmitted. Children absorb how safety is established, how conflict is handled, and what the world expects of them. These lessons are rarely spoken. They are modelled.

A family shaped by scarcity carries vigilance even in abundance.
A family shaped by displacement carries mistrust even in stability.
A family shaped by gratitude carries resilience even under strain.

Faith traditions recognized this intuitively. Ancestral remembrance, blessings, and prohibitions were not superstition—they were early attempts to acknowledge emotional inheritance.

Modern psychology now observes the same patterns without symbolic language.

Communities and Shared Emotional History

What families carry privately, communities carry publicly.

Regions that have endured repeated conflict develop heightened sensitivity to threat. Communities shaped by collective achievement develop confidence that feels natural rather than earned. These traits persist even when original circumstances fade.

This is why people often "feel" history rather than know it.

Faith preserved these emotional memories through ritual, story, and commemoration. Not to glorify the past—but to prevent amnesia. When memory disappears entirely, societies repeat what they no longer recognize.

Gratitude and Trauma as Diverging Paths

Gratitude and trauma operate as two opposing stabilizers.

Trauma narrows attention toward protection. Gratitude widens it toward continuity. Both are adaptive responses—but they shape future behavior very differently.

Communities that ritualized gratitude recovered faster after disruption. Those that ritualized grievance often carried vigilance forward indefinitely.

Faith traditions placed disproportionate emphasis on gratitude not because it was virtuous, but because it prevented trauma from becoming identity.

This distinction matters.

When trauma is acknowledged but not integrated, it becomes grievance. When gratitude is practiced without denial, it becomes resilience.

Collective memory becomes dangerous only when it hardens.

When memory stops being examined, it turns into entitlement or resentment. History becomes justification. Identity becomes defence.

Religion struggled here because it preserved memory without providing tools for reinterpretation. Science now provides those tools—but often without reverence for what memory protects.

What persists across all cultures is this:

Memory does not disappear when ignored.
It reappears as behavior.

Faith was humanity's first attempt to hold this responsibly.

Why This Matters Now

Modern societies are saturated with inherited memory—national, cultural, familial—yet lack the symbolic literacy to recognize it.

People argue beliefs without seeing the emotional history beneath them. They defend identities without understanding the memories those identities protect.

This is why progress stalls.

Without awareness of collective memory, societies repeat what they no longer remember choosing.

The Bridge Forward

Understanding faith as memory preservation reframes it entirely.

It is no longer something to believe or reject.
It becomes something to *interpret.*

And once interpretation begins, another realization follows naturally:

If belief, gratitude, and memory can shape biology and
behavior unconsciously,
what happens when belief itself is examined consciously?

That question leads us toward the closing movement of this book—where faith gives way to responsibility.

Chapter 10
Thought, Emotion, And Energy — What Science Can Now Measure

For centuries, faith spoke of unseen forces shaping human life.
For centuries, science dismissed such claims as metaphor or imagination.

What has changed is not belief.
What has changed is **measurement**.

Modern science has not validated ancient language—but it has begun to observe the mechanisms those languages were attempting to describe.

Thought Is Not Abstract to the Body

Thought does not remain in the mind.

Every sustained pattern of thought produces a corresponding physiological response. Stress alters hormone levels. Calm changes heart rhythms. Anticipation shifts muscle tone. Emotion reorganizes attention.

Neuroscience now shows that the brain does not merely *think*—it coordinates the entire organism.

Thought is information.
Emotion is interpretation.
The body is the medium.

Religious traditions did not speak in these terms, but they organized life around the same understanding: inner state shapes outer reality.

Emotion as Measurable Signal

Emotion is not vague energy. It is a **measurable biological signal**.

Heart-rate variability reflects emotional regulation. Cortisol levels track chronic stress. Immune response correlates with prolonged emotional states. Neural coherence reflects clarity or fragmentation.

These measurements do not explain meaning—but they confirm that **inner states have physical consequences**.

What was once called blessing or imbalance now appears as resilience or dysregulation.

▢ Inner State and Bodily Effect in Texts

- **Christianity:** "A peaceful heart gives life to the body."
- **Islam:** The heart as the center of understanding
- **Hinduism:** *Prana* flowing through the body.
- **Buddhism:** Mind shaping experience
- **Sikhism:** Inner remembrance shaping conduct.

Stress as the Modern Equivalent of Fear

One of the clearest bridges between ancient intuition and modern science is stress.

Chronic stress reproduces the effects of sustained fear—narrowed perception, reduced empathy, impaired judgment. It compromises immunity, accelerates aging, and destabilizes emotion.

Religious emphasis on rest, prayer, fasting, and rhythm was not arbitrary. They interrupted stress cycles.

What was once called spiritual discipline now appears as **physiological regulation**.

Placebo, Expectation, and Meaning

One of the most uncomfortable findings in modern medicine is the placebo effect.

Belief alone—without active intervention—can alter symptoms, pain perception, and recovery trajectories. This does not mean belief creates reality, but it does mean **expectation alters experience**.

Science struggles here because placebo does not fit clean causal models.

Faith never struggled with this. It built entire systems around expectation, trust, and meaning—sometimes wisely, sometimes manipulatively.

☐ **Expectation and Healing in Texts**

- **Christianity:** "Your faith has made you well."
- **Islam:** Healing through trust in God
- **Hinduism:** Faith in ritual and intention
- **Buddhism:** Mindfulness influencing suffering.
- **Sikhism:** Inner alignment preceding action

Why Science Is Careful—and Right to Be

Science avoids language like "energy" not because inner influence is unreal, but because imprecise language invites misuse.

Not everything that feels powerful is measurable. Not everything measurable is meaningful.

This caution is necessary.

At the same time, dismissing inner experience because it resists measurement leaves a gap—one that religion once filled imperfectly.

The challenge now is to speak carefully, not silently.

Why Science Took So Long to Look Inward

Science did not ignore inner experience out of arrogance.

It avoided it out of necessity.

Early scientific progress depended on isolating variables, controlling conditions, and reproducing results. Inner states—thoughts, emotions, expectations—resisted all three. They varied between individuals, shifted over time, and responded to observation itself.

To study the external world effectively, science had to bracket subjectivity.

This decision was methodological, not ideological.

Measurement Required Distance

The early successes of science came from studying systems that behaved consistently regardless of who observed them.

Gravity did not change with mood.
Chemical reactions did not depend on belief.
Mechanical systems responded predictably.

This reliability allowed science to separate observer from observed.

Inner experience did not cooperate.

Thought altered physiology. Emotion changed outcomes. Expectation interfered with results. The observer could not be removed from the experiment.

So, science postponed the problem.

What Changed Was Not Belief, but Tools

The shift toward studying inner states did not occur because science became more open-minded.

It occurred because instrumentation improved.

Brain imaging made neural activity visible. Hormonal assays quantified stress responses. Heart-rate variability provided proxies for emotional regulation. Longitudinal studies revealed patterns invisible in short experiments.

Crucially, these tools did not measure meaning.
They measured *variables correlated with meaning.*

Science did not claim that thought was energy in a mystical sense. It showed that thought has physiological signatures.

This distinction matters.

Why "Energy" Remains a Dangerous Word

Scientific caution around language is often mistaken for denial.

In physics, energy has a precise definition. In human experience, the word is used metaphorically to describe sensation, vitality, or emotional tone. Confusing these domains creates false certainty.

When traditions spoke of energy, they were describing felt coherence, not measurable force.

Science resists this language not because the experience is unreal, but because imprecision invites misuse.

This restraint protects inquiry.

The Placebo Problem That Would Not Disappear

Placebo effects forced science to confront subjectivity.

No matter how tightly controlled experiments became, expectation continued to influence outcome. Attempts to eliminate placebo revealed its persistence.

This did not prove belief creates reality.
It proved belief alters response.

That distinction reshaped medicine, psychology, and neuroscience—slowly and reluctantly.

Science accepted influence without endorsing metaphysics.

Science's current position is therefore careful, not dismissive.

It acknowledges that:

- Inner states influence bodily systems.
- Expectation modulates outcome.
- Regulation affects resilience.

But it refuses to speculate beyond what can be observed.

This restraint is not a weakness.
It is discipline.

What Can Be Said Without Overreach

We can say this with confidence:

- Thought alters physiology.
- Emotion influences perception and behavior
- Meaning shapes endurance and recovery
- Expectation modulates experience.

These are no longer philosophical claims. They are observable patterns.

What remains unresolved is the question of control.

Do these processes unfold automatically, or can they be engaged deliberately?

Faith assumed responsibility without explanation.

Science observes effect without instruction.

The missing link is conscious responsibility.

Why This Moment Matters

At this point in the inquiry, something subtle has shifted.

Faith has been examined without being dismissed. Science has been extended toward experience without being distorted.

What remains is not a conclusion, but a quiet implication:
if thought and emotion shape experience whether they are acknowledged or not,
then attention itself becomes consequential.

This is not a claim about control.
It is an observation about responsibility.

The Question That Follows

This leads naturally to the next inquiry:

If inner states and beliefs influence outcomes,

and if expectation, and meaning alter biology and behavior,

then **what is it that regulates them?**

That question takes us closer to the boundary of this book.

Chapter 11
Consciousness, Placebo, And The Power of Belief

Belief is often treated as a personal choice—something one may adopt or reject.

In practice, belief is unavoidable.

Every human being operates from assumptions about safety, threat, possibility, identity, and outcome. These assumptions may not be articulated, but they shape perception, emotion, and behavior continuously.

The real distinction is not between believers and non-believers. It is between **examined belief and unexamined belief**.

What the Placebo Effect Actually Reveals

The placebo effect is one of the most unsettling findings in modern science.

A substance with no active ingredients can produce measurable changes in pain, recovery, and physiological response—solely because the recipient expects improvement.

This does not imply deception.
It implies influence.

The body responds not only to chemistry, but to **interpretation**.

Medicine attempts to isolate placebo to protect objectivity. Yet its consistent presence reveals something fundamental: meaning alters experience.

Religion built its practices around this reality long before it could be named.

▢ Belief and Outcome in Texts

- **Christianity:** "According to your faith let it be done to you."
- **Islam:** Trust (*tawakkul*) shaping outcome.
- **Hinduism:** Intention (*sankalpa*) preceding action
- **Buddhism:** Mind shaping suffering and release
- **Sikhism:** Inner orientation determining conduct.

Why Belief Works Even When Unacknowledged

Belief does not require conscious endorsement.

Expectations form through memory, conditioning, and emotional experience. A person raised in chronic insecurity carries anticipatory threat into neutral situations. A person raised in safety carries openness without effort.

Neither is choosing their belief.
Both are living it.

This is why belief-based interventions work even when individuals deny believing in them. The nervous system responds to expectation whether the intellect agrees or not.

Consciousness Changes the Equation

The introduction of awareness alters everything.

When belief remains unconscious, it governs behavior invisibly. When belief becomes conscious, it becomes adjustable.

This is the difference between:

- Being driven by fear
- Recognizing fear as a state

Between:

- Acting from habit
- Choosing response

Faith traditions hinted at this through practices of reflection, confession, remembrance, and meditation. Psychology now frames it as metacognition and self-regulation.

The mechanism is the same.

▢ Practices of Awareness

- **Christianity:** Examination of conscience
- **Islam:** Self-accounting (*muhasabah*)
- **Hinduism:** Self-inquiry (*atma vichara*)
- **Buddhism:** Mindfulness
- **Sikhism:** Awareness through *Naam*

The Danger of Blind Belief

Belief without awareness becomes dangerous.

Unquestioned belief fuels fanaticism, fear-based obedience, and identity conflict. History offers countless examples—not because belief is inherently destructive, but because **belief without consciousness resists correction**.

This is where religion failed its own insight.

It preserved belief but discouraged examination.

Belief as Expectation, Not Force

Belief does not operate by altering reality directly.

It operates by altering expectation, and expectation shapes how the nervous system allocates attention, energy, and response.

This distinction matters.

When belief is treated as a force, it drifts into superstition. When it is understood as expectation, it becomes observable, measurable, and limited — yet undeniably influential.

The Brain as a Prediction Engine

Modern neuroscience increasingly describes the brain as predictive rather than reactive.

At every moment, the brain generates expectations about what will happen next. Sensory input is then interpreted in light of these predictions. When expectation and input align, experience feels stable. When they conflict, the brain adjusts.

Belief enters here — not as certainty, but as *prior expectation.*

Strong expectations bias interpretation. They influence pain perception, immune response, stress regulation, and recovery. This does not mean belief creates outcomes freely. It means belief shapes response within constraints.

Why Placebo Works — and Why It Fails

Placebo effects do not prove that belief heals everything.

They prove that expectation alters physiological response.

Perceived pain diminishes. Stress hormones reduce. Immune markers shift modestly. These effects are real, repeatable, and bounded.

Placebo does not regenerate organs.
It does not override advanced pathology.
It does not suspend biological limits.

What it does is remove internal resistance that would otherwise worsen outcomes.

This is why placebo effects are most evident in areas where physiological regulation plays a central role — pain, fatigue, anxiety, and the process of recovery.

The Nocebo Mirror

If expectation can ease symptoms, it can also amplify them.

Nocebo effects demonstrate the same mechanism in reverse. Negative expectation increases pain, side effects, and perceived dysfunction.

This is not weakness.
It is sensitivity.

The nervous system responds to anticipated threat by tightening, preparing, and protecting — often at a cost.

Faith traditions intuited this when they warned against despair and chronic fear. Psychology now measures it without moral framing.

Repetition, Ritual, and Reinforcement

Belief rarely operates through single decisions.

It operates through repetition.

Repeated expectations strengthen predictive models. Rituals, affirmations, and repeated narratives work not because they are magical, but because they stabilize expectation over time.

This is why rituals existed long before science could explain them.

The danger begins when repetition replaces reflection. When belief hardens without awareness, it resists correction.

This is where faith becomes fragile.

Why Belief Cannot Replace Awareness

Belief alone is unstable.

When challenged, it collapses or becomes defensive. Awareness, by contrast, adapts. It allows expectation to update rather than entrench.

This is why belief without awareness becomes dependency.

Faith traditions that survived longest paired belief with humility, doubt, and self-examination — even if later interpretations obscured this balance.

Science insists on this balance explicitly.

The Danger of Denying Belief

Denial is not neutrality.

When belief is dismissed rather than examined, it continues to operate unchecked. Skepticism that ignores inner conditioning leaves emotional patterns intact while claiming rational superiority.

This produces a different form of blindness.

Science often errs here—not by studying belief, but by pretending it does not matter outside placebo controls.

Responsibility Emerges with Awareness

Once belief is recognized as influential, responsibility follows naturally.

If expectation shapes experience, then cultivating clarity is no longer optional. Emotional regulation becomes ethical. Awareness becomes a form of stewardship.

This is not moral pressure.
It is causal reality.

Belief, then, is neither illusion nor power.

It is a tuning mechanism — one that can assist or distort depending on how consciously it is held.

Understanding this prepares us to explore a subtler question:

How does the mind project possibility forward — not just through belief, but through imagination, memory, and dreams?

That is where we turn next.

What Faith Pointed Toward — and Stopped Short Of

Faith traditions recognized belief's power but externalized authority. Science recognizes belief's effect but avoids instruction.

What remains unaddressed is **how individuals consciously engage belief without surrendering autonomy**.

That question lies just beyond this chapter.

A Shift in Emphasis

At this point in the inquiry, something has quietly changed.

Faith has been examined without being dismissed.
Science has been extended toward experience without overreach.
Belief has been recognized as unavoidable.

What begins to emerge is a deeper question — not yet about answers, but about participation:

If belief operates continuously,
and if awareness alters its effect,
then what role does deliberate self-observation play in shaping experience?

That question reshapes the direction of the inquiry.

Interlude II
Power, Fear, And the Discipline Of Not Knowing

How Authority Replaced Insight — and Why Humility Is the Only Way Forward

---

Why This Interlude Exists

Up to this point, the book has explored how belief, emotion, memory, and awareness shape human experience from within.

What has not yet been examined directly is what happens when these inner forces scale—when they move beyond individuals and become embedded in systems, traditions, and authority.

This interlude exists to address that moment.

Not to accuse.
Not to dismantle faith.
Not to glorify science.

But to observe a repeating human pattern with honesty and restraint.

The Central Observation

Across cultures and centuries, one truth appears again and again:

Fear is more efficient than understanding.

It coordinates behavior faster.
It simplifies complexity.
It discourages dissent.

For small groups, this can be adaptive.
For large systems, it becomes irresistible.

This is not a failure of religion or politics alone.
It is a structural tendency of human organization.

How Insight Becomes Authority

Every major tradition begins with lived insight.

Someone sees clearly.
Others recognize the clarity.
A community forms.

At this stage, guidance remains flexible. Meaning is contextual. Authority serves understanding.

But as numbers grow, something shifts.

Experience is hard to standardize.
Awareness is unpredictable.
Fear, by contrast, is reliable.

So systems slowly pivot—from guidance to governance.

This shift rarely feels oppressive from the inside.

It feels necessary.

Christianity

Salvation, Damnation, and the Governance of Fear

Early Christian teachings emphasized inner transformation: love, forgiveness, humility, and compassion as lived states.

The "Kingdom of God" was described as *within*, not external. Parables were used precisely because direct instruction could not transmit inner change.

As Christianity scaled, inner states became moral categories. Salvation and damnation—once symbolic of psychological orientation—became tools of order.

Fear of eternal consequence replaced responsibility for present awareness.

This did not begin as manipulation.
It began as administration.

Islam

Law, Order, and the Strain Between Mercy and Control

Islam articulated a powerful inner principle: *tawhid*—unity of orientation.

Submission (*Islam*) was meant to reduce inner fragmentation, aligning intention, action, and awareness.

As Islamic societies expanded, law (*Sharia*) became necessary for coherence. Over time, clarity hardened where mercy (*rahma*) required interpretation.

Fear of transgression proved easier to govern than cultivation of inner alignment.

Sufi traditions preserved the experiential core—but often at the margins of authority.

Hinduism

Cosmic Order and Social Fixation

Hindu philosophy approached reality symbolically, describing inner dynamics through cosmology, myth, and metaphor.

Dharma was alignment with reality—not obedience.

When symbolic cosmology intersected with social order, metaphor hardened into hierarchy. What was descriptive became prescriptive.

Fear of social consequence replaced responsibility for inner clarity.

The insight endured.
The structure distorted.

Buddhism

Discipline Without Coercion — and Its Limits

Buddhism offered one of the most psychologically precise maps of suffering.

Attachment, not circumstance, was identified as the root of distress. Liberation was experiential, not granted.

Yet even here, institutions emerged. Lineage replaced inquiry. Discipline sometimes replaced direct seeing.

Fear was subtle—fear of deviation, fear of impurity, fear of error.

No system, however careful, is immune to organizational gravity.

Sikhism

Authority Grounded in Fearlessness

Sikhism arose explicitly against fear-based domination.

Its emphasis on *nirbhau* (fearlessness), dignity, and service insisted that clarity must survive ordinary life—not retreat from it.

Authority was meant to serve awareness, not replace it.

Yet even here, constant renewal was required to prevent discipline from hardening into identity.

The Pattern Beneath the Traditions

Across traditions, the sequence repeats:

1. Insight emerges
2. Community forms
3. Structure stabilizes
4. Fear simplifies governance
5. Authority detaches from awareness

This is not moral collapse.
It is organizational gravity.

Fear scales.
Clarity resists scripting.

Why Power Prefers Fear

Integrated individuals are difficult to control.

They tolerate ambiguity.
They ask inconvenient questions.
They do not require constant reassurance.

Fear, by contrast:

- Produces compliance
- Rewards conformity
- Encourages self-policing

Power does not need cruelty to function this way.
It needs only scale and uncertainty.

The Modern Echo

This pattern did not end with religion.

It reappears wherever:

- Metrics replace meaning
- Loyalty replaces understanding
- Identity replaces inquiry
- Stability is prioritized over truth

The vocabulary changes.
The mechanism does not.

Where Both Faith and Science Went Too Far

Faith faltered when symbols were mistaken for conclusions.

Science falters when measurement is mistaken for total explanation.

Both fail when certainty outruns humility.

Faith once preserved insight without mechanism.
Science preserves mechanism without meaning.

Neither alone is sufficient.

The Discipline of Not Knowing

Humility is not self-doubt.

It is a sense of scale.

It recognizes that:

- Experience precedes explanation
- Influence exists before mechanism
- Meaning often arrives before language

Science institutionalizes humility by insisting on testable claims and defined boundaries.
Faith once did so through symbol.

Both lose integrity when they claim closure too soon.

The Cost of Premature Certainty

When belief overextends, people feel responsible for outcomes they cannot control.
When science overextends, people feel reduced to mechanisms they do not recognize.

Both forms of certainty cause harm—quietly.

History is filled with confident explanations later revealed to be partial.

The discipline is not to avoid conclusion entirely.
It is to hold conclusions lightly.

Why This Matters Before Dreams and Possibility

The next chapter explores imagination, memory, and future projection.

This terrain is especially vulnerable.

Without humility:

- Dreams become prophecy
- Imagination becomes entitlement
- Possibility becomes illusion

With humility:

- Dreams inform
- Imagination explores
- Possibility invites responsibility

This distinction determines whether insight integrates or destabilizes.

A Final Orientation

The most mature position between faith and science is not synthesis.

It is restraint.

To observe without rushing to conclude.
To remain open without becoming unanchored.
To recognize influence without claiming control.

Not knowing is not failure.

It is the condition under which understanding continues to grow.

Chapter 12
Dreams, Memory, And Future Possibility

Human beings do not move into the future empty-handed.

They carry memory.

Not only remembered events, but emotional residues, unfinished patterns, unresolved fears, and unfulfilled possibilities. These do not remain confined to the past. They shape anticipation, expectation, and choice—often without awareness.

Dreams sit at the intersection of this process.

They are not prophecies.
They are not messages from elsewhere.
They are **integration**.

What Dreams Actually Do

Neuroscience understands dreams as integrative activity.

During sleep, especially in rapid eye movement (REM) states, the brain revisits memory fragments, emotional signals, and incomplete narratives. It recombines them, testing possibilities without external consequence.

Dreams are not random.
They are *reorganizational.*

They allow the mind to explore future outcomes using past material. This is why dreams often blend memory with imagination, fear with hope, and familiarity with novelty.

Religious traditions treated dreams with seriousness not because they predicted fate—but because they revealed **direction**.

▢ Dreams in Religious Texts

- **Christianity:** Joseph's dreams guiding action
- **Islam:** Dreams as one part of revelation
- **Hinduism:** Dreams as reflections of *vasanas* (latent tendencies)
- **Buddhism:** Dreams as mental formations
- **Sikhism:** Awareness transcending waking and dreaming states

---

Memory as the Raw Material of Experience

The future does not emerge from nothing.

It is constructed from memory—what is remembered, what is avoided, and what remains unresolved. Dreams expose this process because they are not filtered by social performance or rational justification.

What appears symbolically at night often operates silently during the day.

Unexamined memory repeats itself as habit.
Examined memory transforms into possibility.

This is why traditions encouraged reflection, journaling, prayer, and contemplation. These were not acts of devotion alone—they were methods of **pattern recognition**.

How the Mind Rehearses the Future

Dreams are often treated as messages to be decoded.

This framing is understandable, but incomplete.

Dreams are not communications from outside the mind. They are internal simulations — the mind's way of integrating memory, emotion, and possibility when conscious control is reduced.

They do not predict the future.
They *prepare* for it.

Memory as the Basis of Possibility

The mind cannot imagine from nothing.

Every image, scenario, or narrative that appears in dreams is assembled from fragments of past experience — memories, emotions, unresolved tensions, and incomplete patterns.

What makes dreams feel unfamiliar is not their origin, but their recombination.

The brain explores variations without the constraints of waking logic. It tests emotional responses, rehearses outcomes, and surfaces conflicts that were suppressed during the day.

This is not symbolism imposed by meaning.
It is meaning emerging from memory.

Emotion, Not Logic, Drives Dream Formation

Dreams are not organized around rational sequence.

They are organized around emotional salience.

Unresolved fear, anticipation, hope, guilt, or curiosity pulls memory fragments into coherence. The dream does not explain these emotions — it *expresses* them.

This is why attempts to interpret dreams literally fail. The same image can arise from entirely different emotional states in different people.

What matters is not *what appears*, but *what is being rehearsed emotionally*.

Imagination as a Future-Simulation Engine

During waking life, imagination continues the same function more deliberately.

The mind projects scenarios forward, evaluates risk, anticipates response, and adjusts behavior accordingly. This is how humans prepare for uncertainty.

When imagination is grounded, it enables planning and creativity.
When it is untethered, it becomes fantasy or anxiety.

Dreams sit between these two states — less constrained than imagination, more grounded than fantasy.

They are rehearsal without commitment.

Why Cultures Treated Dreams as Sacred

Before neuroscience, dreams were one of the few observable windows into inner life.

They felt autonomous.
They carried emotional weight.
They arrived without effort.

Cultures treated them as sacred not because they were prophetic, but because they revealed unconscious processing long before that term existed.

The error came later — when dreams were treated as instruction rather than information.

Responsibility in Shaping Possibility

Dreams do not determine the future.

They reflect the direction of inner attention.

A mind saturated with fear rehearses threat.
A mind anchored in gratitude rehearses continuity.
A mind fragmented rehearses instability.

This does not mean thoughts create reality freely.
It means attention conditions readiness.

The future emerges from action — but action is shaped by what the mind repeatedly rehearses.

Understanding this restores responsibility without mysticism.

It suggests that the most influential future-shaping act is not prediction, but attention discipline.

What you dwell on repeatedly becomes familiar.
What becomes familiar feels inevitable.

Dreams reveal what the mind is practicing.

The Danger of Interpreting Without Awareness

Dreams were often misused.

Taken literally, they became superstition. Taken authoritatively, they became control mechanisms. Taken as destiny, they removed responsibility.

The insight was never that dreams dictate the future. The insight was that **they reveal the mind preparing for it**.

Modern psychology echoes this understanding, though without symbolic language.

Hope and Fear as Future-Shaping Forces

Dreams reveal something else clearly: the future is emotionally biased.

A mind anchored in fear dreams differently from one anchored in safety. Hope expands possibility; fear narrows it. This pattern extends beyond sleep into waking life.

People do not move toward the future they desire. They move toward the future they expect.

Faith traditions spoke of hope as virtue not because it was comforting—but because it altered trajectory.

▢ Hope and Orientation in Texts

- **Christianity:** Faith as assurance of unseen outcomes
- **Islam:** Trust in unfolding (*tawakkul*)
- **Hinduism:** *Shraddha* (orientation of trust)
- **Buddhism:** Right intention
- **Sikhism:** Living without fear of tomorrow

Why the Future Feels Uncertain

The future feels uncertain because awareness is partial.

The mind senses possibility but lacks clarity. Dreams attempt to bridge this gap by simulating outcomes. When awareness increases, anxiety often decreases—not because the future becomes predictable, but because the mind becomes less fragmented.

Faith once provided this anchoring externally.
Science provides prediction externally.
Neither addresses the **internal orientation** fully.

That is the task now.

The Quiet Transition

This chapter marks a subtle shift.

Up to this point, *Faith Misunderstood* has focused on:

- Explaining why faith emerged
- How it preserved meaning

- Where it distorted
- What science now confirms

What remains is not belief—but **responsibility**.

If memory shapes the future,
if belief influences outcome,
if awareness alters interpretation,
then the next step is no longer philosophical.

It is practical.

Approaching the Edge

Faith Misunderstood does not end with answers meant to control the mind,
or techniques designed to master thought,
or promises of liberation.

Those concerns lie beyond the scope of this chapter.

What this inquiry has aimed to do instead is more modest and more foundational:
to clear the ground — to loosen fear, restore dignity to questioning, and allow science and inner experience to coexist without distortion.

What follows requires a different kind of readiness.

If thought, emotion, belief, and memory shape life whether they are acknowledged or not,
then the remaining question is not whether they influence experience,
but how they are lived with.

The chapters ahead explore this boundary carefully —
where understanding deepens,
and responsibility quietly begins to take shape.

Chapter 13
Faith Without Dependency

Faith becomes dangerous the moment it replaces responsibility.

This danger does not come from belief itself, but from **surrendering responsibility** for one's inner life to something outside oneself—an authority, a system, a doctrine, or even an idea.

What began as guidance slowly becomes dependency.

When Faith Crosses the Line

Faith was originally meant to support inner alignment. Dependency shifts that alignment outward.

Instead of asking:

- *What am I seeing?*
- *What am I feeling?*
- *What is this experience revealing?*

The dependent mind asks:

- *What am I supposed to believe?*
- *What is permitted?*
- *Who decides what is true?*

This shift appears subtle, but it changes everything.

Ownership of one's inner life dissolves quietly.

Why Dependency Feels Comforting

Dependency offers relief.

It removes uncertainty.
It distributes responsibility.
It promises safety through obedience.

For minds overwhelmed by fear or instability, this can be temporarily stabilizing. That is why dependency is not inherently malicious—it often begins as **psychological shelter**.

But shelter is not a home.

What protects you during a storm cannot be lived in permanently.

The Cost of Surrendered Responsibility

When responsibility for one's inner life is outsourced, growth stalls.

Moral responsibility becomes compliance.
Curiosity becomes doubt.
Awareness becomes loyalty.

Over time, individuals lose confidence in their own perception. They begin to mistrust insight unless it is externally validated. This creates a subtle fragility—one that reacts defensively to challenge and clings to certainty.

Faith then stops pointing inward and begins policing outward.

▢ Dependency Warnings Across Traditions

- **Christianity:** "The letter kills, but the Spirit gives life."
- **Islam:** No compulsion in faith
- **Hinduism:** Truth realized, not inherited
- **Buddhism:** Do not accept teachings blindly
- **Sikhism:** Blind ritual without understanding is empty

Faith as Inner Clarity

At its healthiest, faith was never submission to authority.

It was confidence in **inner coherence**.

Faith meant:

- Trusting clarity over impulse
- Choosing alignment over reaction
- Acting without fear of uncertainty

This kind of faith does not need defence.
It does not fear questions.
It does not require identity.

It is quiet, grounded, and internally anchored.

Why Systems Resist This Form of Faith

Inner clarity cannot be controlled.

It does not scale easily.
It does not submit predictably.
It cannot be monopolized.

Systems prefer dependency because dependency is manageable. Clarity is not.

This is why teachings that emphasized awareness, inquiry, and direct experience were often softened, ritualized, or marginalized.

Not because they were wrong—but because they were **inconvenient**.

The Turning Point

There comes a moment—often subtle—when faith stops being helpful.

Not because it fails, but because it has done its job.

At that moment, clinging to faith becomes hesitation.

The individual senses this intuitively:

- The answers no longer satisfy
- The rituals feel hollow
- The questions deepen rather than resolve

This is not loss of faith.
It is **maturation**.

Where Dependency Hides Today

Dependency did not vanish when faith weakened.

It simply changed form.

When belief systems lose authority, the human need for certainty does not disappear. It relocates—to new figures, new institutions, and new explanations that promise safety without demanding inner work.

What looks like progress often conceals the same psychological pattern.

You can see this in how people relate to expertise.

Science, which began as a method of inquiry, is often treated as a source of certainty. Data is cited without understanding. Conclusions are repeated without context. Complexity is reduced to slogans.

The question quietly shifts from *"What does this evidence suggest?"*
to *"What am I allowed to think?"*

This is not respect for science.
It is dependency wearing a rational face.

You see it in leadership and ideology.

Political movements, social identities, and moral causes increasingly function as substitutes for belief. They offer belonging, certainty, and moral clarity—often at the cost of nuance and self-examination.

Individuals outsource judgment to group consensus. Dissent feels dangerous. Curiosity feels disloyal.

Faith has not disappeared here.
It has been **reassigned**.

You see it in personal development and spirituality itself.

Teachers become authorities. Practices become prescriptions. Language becomes identity. The promise of clarity slowly shifts into the demand for adherence.

What began as exploration becomes conformity.

Dependency is subtle precisely because it feels reassuring.

Even psychology and mental health are not immune.

Diagnostic language can become identity. Labels can replace inquiry. Relief comes not from understanding patterns, but from locating responsibility elsewhere.

Support becomes dependency when awareness is no longer encouraged.

The common thread across these domains is not belief—it is **avoidance of uncertainty**.

True responsibility requires tolerance for ambiguity. It requires the ability to hold not-knowing without immediately reaching for authority.

Dependency resolves discomfort quickly.
Clarity resolves it slowly.

This is why faith, when misunderstood, becomes dangerous—not because it is wrong, but because it is **prematurely final**.

When answers arrive before awareness matures, growth stops.

Recognizing dependency does not require rejection.

It requires honesty.

To ask, quietly and without judgment:

- *Where have I stopped looking for myself?*
- *Where have I outsourced understanding?*
- *Where does certainty feel safer than clarity?*

These questions are not accusations.
They are invitations back to responsibility.

This reorientation does not require abandoning faith, science, or structure.

It requires **repositioning them**.

From authority → reference
From command → context
From certainty → orientation

Standing at the Edge

To stand at the edge of faith is uncomfortable.

There is no authority to lean on.
No doctrine to hide behind.
No belief to defend.

Only awareness remains.

This is where faith either tightens into dependency—or loosens into understanding.

Chapter 14
The Quiet Realization

The end of faith does not arrive with drama.

It arrives quietly.

Not as disbelief.
Not as rebellion.
But as **understanding**.

When Belief Is No Longer Needed

Belief exists to bridge uncertainty.

Once understanding stabilizes, belief becomes redundant—not false, but unnecessary.

You do not *believe* the ground will hold you.
You walk.

You do not *believe* awareness exists.
You experience it.

This is the quiet realization faith was always pointing toward.

The Dissolving of Effort

At this stage, something unexpected happens.

The effort to believe fades.
The effort to convince disappears.
The effort to defend vanishes.

Clarity no longer feels like achievement.
It feels like **absence of noise**.

Fear does not disappear—but it is seen.
Thought does not stop—but it is observed.
Emotion still arises—but it no longer overwhelms.

Awareness Without Identity

One of the most subtle shifts here is the loss of spiritual identity.

There is no longer a need to be:

- A believer
- A seeker
- A skeptic
- An awakened person

Identity dissolves because it is no longer useful.

What remains is responsiveness.

> **☐ Silence Beyond Belief**
>
> - **Christianity:** "Be still and know."
> - **Islam:** Surrender without fear
> - **Hinduism:** *Neti, neti*
> - **Buddhism:** Emptiness (*Shunyata*)
> - **Sikhism:** Stillness in remembrance

Why This Feels Like an Ending

Faith often provided meaning, structure, and reassurance.

When it dissolves, there can be a sense of loss—not of truth, but of **support**.

This loss is natural.

What is ending is not meaning—but **dependency on meaning**.

The Beginning Hidden Inside the End

What emerges in place of belief is not certainty.

It is **responsibility**.

Responsibility for:

- One's thoughts
- One's emotional patterns
- One's reactions
- One's influence on others

Nothing external guarantees outcomes anymore.

And paradoxically, this is liberating.

Why This Is Not the End of the Journey

This book stops here deliberately.

Awareness has been restored.
Belief has been recontextualized.
Faith has completed its role.

What has *not* yet been addressed is **how awareness is sustained**, **how thought is observed**, and **how emotion is regulated consciously**.

Those are not philosophical questions.

They are practical ones.

The Threshold

If you have reached this point without urgency, without excitement, and without fear—only with a quiet sense of readiness—then you are standing at the threshold.

Not of belief.
Not of faith.
But of **deliberate awareness**.

That threshold is the Final Frontier.

Epilogue

When Faith Steps Aside

Faith was never the destination.
It was a bridge.

A bridge across fear, uncertainty, and fragmentation—built at a time when humanity lacked the language, tools, and self-understanding to cross any other way.

For centuries, that bridge carried people forward. It preserved meaning. It stabilized societies. It softened suffering where explanation was absent. Without faith, much of humanity would not have endured long enough to question it.

But bridges are not meant to be lived on.

What Faith Did Right

Faith gave humans permission to look inward when the world felt overwhelming. It offered hope when control was impossible. It reminded people that inner life mattered long before psychology recognized it.

At its best, faith:

- Reduced fear
- Encouraged compassion
- Created continuity
- Preserved inner questions across generations

None of this was accidental.

Faith was an intelligent response to an immature understanding of consciousness.

What Faith Could Not Do

Faith could not teach responsibility for awareness.

It could point.
It could guide.
It could stabilize.

But it could not replace the work of observing one's own thoughts, emotions, and reactions directly. Where faith became permanent, growth stalled. Where belief replaced understanding, dependency followed.

This was not betrayal.
It was limitation.

Every tool has its scope.

The Moment Faith Steps Aside

Faith steps aside not when it is rejected—but when it is **no longer needed**.

This moment does not arrive through argument or rebellion. It arrives through quiet clarity. Through noticing patterns. Through recognizing how belief has shaped perception, behavior, and choice.

At that moment, faith loosens its grip naturally.

What remains is not disbelief, but **direct engagement** with experience.

Science, Faith, and the Human Future

Science will continue refining its understanding of the external world. Faith will continue offering symbolic language to those who need it.

Neither needs to defeat the other.

What matters now is something else entirely: whether individuals are willing to take responsibility for their inner world with the same seriousness they apply to the outer one.

The future of humanity will not be decided by belief systems or technologies alone—but by the level of awareness with which humans use them.

A Final Clarification

This book did not ask you to believe differently.

It asked you to **see differently**.

If faith helped you see more clearly, it served its purpose. If it no longer does, it is not an enemy—it has fulfilled its role.

Where This Leaves You

There is nothing to adopt after this book.
Nothing to join.
Nothing to defend.

Only something to notice.

Thoughts arise.
Emotions follow.
Reactions cascade.
Consequences accumulate.

Most of life unfolds here—quietly, habitually, unconsciously.

The next step is not faith.
It is **attention**.

The Open Door

If you feel no urgency to move forward, pause here. Integration takes time.

If you feel curiosity without excitement, steadiness without certainty, and responsibility without fear—then the door ahead is already open.

The work beyond this point is not about belief or meaning.

It is about **learning to observe the mind as it operates**, moment by moment, without avoidance and without indulgence.

That exploration lies beyond faith – at the final frontier of direct inner engagement.

Where You're Now

You do not need to decide anything after finishing this book.

Nothing here requires agreement, adoption, or action.

If faith once provided structure, it may now feel quieter—or unchanged. Both are valid.

If some ideas felt clarifying, and others felt distant or unnecessary, that is expected. This book was not written to replace belief, but to reposition it.

You may notice one of three things:

- Faith feels less urgent, but not absent
- Questions feel clearer, but not resolved
- A quiet sense of responsibility has replaced certainty

None of these require movement.

At some point, further inquiry may turn away from meaning or reassurance and toward direct attention — how thought forms, how emotion is regulated, and how inner experience is engaged moment by moment. Without readiness, this can feel abstract or demanding.

If curiosity is calm rather than restless, and there is no impulse to seek answers immediately, you are exactly where you need to be.

And if these ideas feel unsettled or incomplete, there is no urgency to move forward.

Clarity unfolds in its own time.